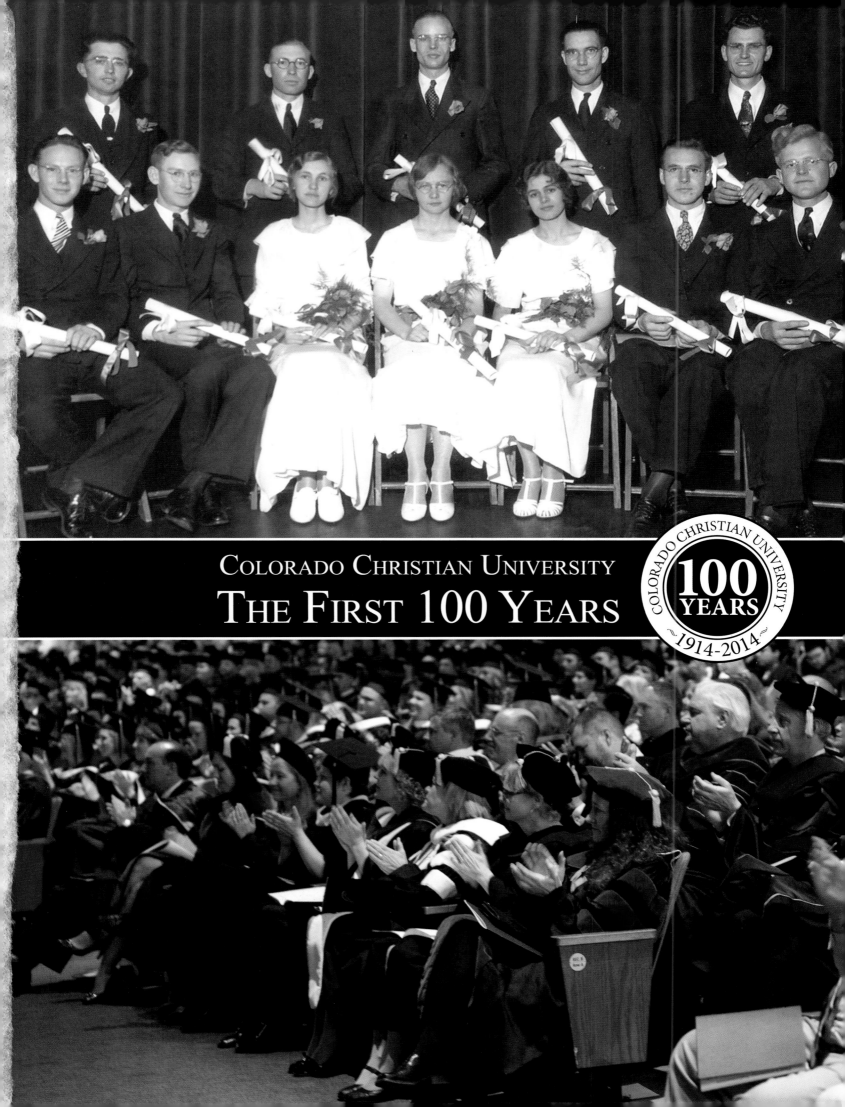

Colorado Christian University
The First 100 Years

COLORADO CHRISTIAN UNIVERSITY
100 YEARS
1914-2014

Denver Bible Institute (DBI)

DBI becomes Rockmont College

Western Bible Institute (WBI)

Rockmont and WBI merge to become Colorado Christian College

Colorado Baptist University (CBU)

CCC and CBU merge to become Colorado Christian University

COLORADO CHRISTIAN UNIVERSITY
THE FIRST 100 YEARS

by

Janet M. Black, PhD

DENVER BIBLE INSTITUTE

Colorado Christian University
8787 West Alameda Avenue
Lakewood, CO 80226

303-963-3000 or 1-800-44-FAITH

www.ccu.edu

THE
DONNING COMPANY
PUBLISHERS

The Donning Company Publishers
184 Business Park Drive, Suite 206
Virginia Beach, VA 23462

Steve Mull, General Manager
Barbara Buchanan, Office Manager
Anne Burns, Editor
Chad H. Casey, Graphic Designer
Kathy Adams, Imaging Artist
Katie Gardner, Project Research Coordinator and Marketing Advisor
Nathan Stufflebean, Research and Marketing Supervisor

Cathleen Norman, Project Director

Cataloging-in-Publication Data available from the Library of Congress
ISBN: 978-1-57864-893-1

Printed in the United States of America at Walsworth Publishing Company

CONTENTS

FOREWORD

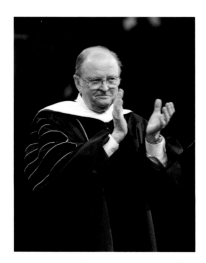

I arrived for work early on the morning of August 22, 2006, my first day as president of Colorado Christian University, with a great sense of destiny for the task to which God had called me—the opportunity to help recruit, pray for, disciple, and educate outstanding students to prepare them for positions of leadership in church, family, academia, business, the arts and professions, politics, military service, and more.

I was also enthusiastic about being part of a community of Christian scholars, staff, trustees, and alumni in an institution, which God had richly blessed over a long period of time. Although there was much about CCU that I did not yet know, I was already well aware of His intervention to preserve and strengthen the university and its heritage institutions from the earliest days in 1914 when it was founded as Denver Bible Institute with a single classroom on Glenarm Street in downtown Denver, two students, and one faculty member.

Nearly eight years later, I have an even more intense appreciation of what God is doing in and through Colorado Christian University. The success He has granted CCU is truly extraordinary:

- Enrollments are soaring, at a time when most private colleges and universities are flat or declining. With 1,110 students on our Lakewood campus and 4,197 students in the university's College of Adult and Graduate Studies (CAGS), we are now a university of 5,307 students.

- Academic standards are now far above most public and private schools. Incoming students in our College of Undergraduate Studies (CCU's traditional program for eighteen to twenty-two year olds) brought with them ACT scores averaging 24.3, up from ACT 21 just a few years earlier.

- Recently, the American Council of Trustees and Alumni (ACTA) reviewed 1,070 U.S. institutions of higher learning, including all the famous schools, public and private. ACTA gave a letter grade to each school based on the content of its general education curriculum. CCU was one of just twenty-one schools to earn an "A."

- CCU's new dual credit program enrolls 1,475 high school juniors and seniors in special classes for which they earn college credit in fifty-one high schools from coast to coast.

- The university has begun new undergraduate and graduate programs in nursing, political science, computer information systems, biblical studies, criminal justice, and other disciplines.

- In its centennial year, CCU will award $12 million in scholarships.

- CCU was named a Top Conservative College by the Young America's Foundation.

- Two hundred and three students are participating in varsity sports.

- In its second and third years, CCU's debate team won the National Christian College Tournament and is scoring victories all over the country.

- Our new Employment Management Service is placing hundreds of students in full and part-time jobs.

- CCU's Centennial Institute is emerging as a national brand, an intellectual powerhouse that brings great scholars, speakers, authors, and activists to campus. Centennial's 2013 Western Conservative Summit broke all records for substance, content, enthusiasm, and attendance—over two thousand attended the fourth annual WCS conference.

- The Lakewood City Council has given the university zoning approval to increase our Lakewood campus from 170,000 square feet to 700,000 square feet. We are in the process of rebuilding the entire campus. We will move into our first new building—43,000 square feet of excellent classrooms and offices—in May 2014, our centennial year.

Much of the credit for these wonderful trends goes to the university's dedicated faculty, staff, and trustees, many of whom have invested decades of their lives in our students. Their faithful testimony and service are truly an inspiration. It is a great honor for me to work with these outstanding men and women.

We thank God, too, for wonderful friends whose financial support has meant so much to this institution and its students. In recent years, more than 22,000 individuals and foundations have made gifts to the university to support scholarships, rebuild our campus, and other purposes. Among these are a handful of exceptionally generous friends who have made very large gifts for which we are eternally grateful. Their impact on the future of CCU is enormous.

Ultimately, of course, all glory belongs to God. To Him we give our utmost appreciation and reserve for Him our highest admiration and loyalty.

As Colorado Christian University begins its second century, we are more focused than ever before on lifting up Jesus, proclaiming the truth of Scripture and championing faith, family, and freedom for our country. God is calling CCU to greatness, to help raise up a generation of men and women who will honor Him and restore the traditional values that make America, for all its flaws and shortcomings, a great, free, prosperous, and generous country.

In this wonderful book, Dr. Janet Black recounts the story of how God has given favor to Colorado Christian University over and over again. Sometimes against formidable odds, the university has survived and prospered and is gaining national recognition. God seems to be saying, "**I will show the world what I will do for a university that honors Me**."

By the grace of God, may we always do so.

William L. Armstrong
President
Colorado Christian University

ACKNOWLEDGMENTS

Thousands of stories, hopes, frustrations, and successes go into making institutions, and this book has benefited from interviews with board members, notably the late Stan Harwood; faculty, staff, and administrators, including the late Dr. Beckman; alumni who keep tabs on others, including Tom Graham and Hazel Parcel; dozens of readers and research assistants; children and grandchildren of institutional VIPs; friends of CCU, such as Ken Gire who conducted videotaped interviews; archivists such as Sandra Brown at Southwest Baptist University: and the always helpful librarians at the Clifton Fowler Library at CCU. Thank you all for your willing responses and timely advice.

I also wish to thank my CCU students who endured numerous second-hand stories, colleagues who delighted in choice anecdotes, and my ever-supportive family.

CHAPTER 1

Formation:
The Denver Bible Institute
1914–1919

Colorado Christian University celebrates a rich history, with three heritage schools joining together to form one strong educational community in the 1980s. Each of the heritage schools has a story to tell; each points to the marvelous grace of the Lord Jesus Christ working through individuals—dedicated visionaries, gifted teachers and students—who creatively pioneered Christian education in the Rocky Mountain region.

Clifton Fowler.

Clifton L. Fowler, Founder

Clifton LeFevre Fowler was born on August 7, 1882, in Kirksville, Missouri, and grew up in St. Louis. Two events shook young Clifton's life: when he was four, his father died; and when he was ten, his mother, who had remarried, sent him to live with his grandmother.

Fowler's grandmother regularly took him to church activities and to hear visiting preachers. When Fowler was fourteen, he was touched by the preaching of D. L. Moody. When he was nineteen, Fowler attended a Bible study at the YMCA. After the meeting, around midnight, Fowler committed his life to Christ.

As a result, Clifton quit his job at the bank where he worked and went on staff with the YMCA. When persistent respiratory problems plagued him, the administrator at the Y sent him to Denver, a drier climate, on a leave of absence. Later, Fowler learned the position he had held in St. Louis was closed. An entrepreneur, Fowler started a restaurant, but when an extended eye infection kept him from business, he lost his restaurant.

From the brokenness of physical and financial collapse, Fowler returned to vocational ministry. Under the umbrella of the Methodist Church, he was charged with reviving a run-down mission. However, because Fowler believed in the "premillennial and literal return of the Lord Jesus"—which caused an uproar among his Methodist colleagues—Fowler was labeled a heretic. Then as he gained counsel from like-minded Christian servants, he followed his call to start a Bible institute in Denver.

DBI and the Bible Institute Movement

D. L. Moody's flagship school, Moody Bible Institute, was founded in 1886. In 1914, DBI joined the nearly twenty-five Bible institutes recently founded in the U.S. and Canada, and by the mid-twentieth century, it was one of more than 250 Bible institutes and colleges in North America.

Fowler approached his venture in an accelerated fashion: while Moody built up momentum through Sunday Bible Classes and seven years of May Institutes taught by Emma Dryer, Fowler started DBI and founded his Sunday Afternoon Bible Class at nearly the same time. Fowler also founded a printing department and an Evening School, following Moody's lead.

While Moody would not open his school until he had donations totaling $250,000, a multi-story classroom building, and donor-sponsored tuition for every student, Fowler rented two humble buildings and engaged a network of friends and supporters to assist in the work. Fowler's vision and energy compelled many to work without remuneration, to live sacrificially in order to train and send out many Christian workers.

In January 1940, Fowler published a *Grace and Truth* article on the legacy of the movement: "When Satan brought Modernism to its finest expression, God prepared for the proclamation of the message of His love. When Satan clarified Modernism, God opened a Bible Institute....The Bible Institute movement, with its growing training centers and its far-flung battle line of fearless Gospel ministers and godly missionaries, is heaven's answer to Modernism."

By the time the Bible college movement reached its one-hundredth anniversary, Bible colleges had an accrediting agency, the American Association of Bible Colleges, and a solid reputation for sending out over 50 percent of American missionaries on the mission field at that time.[1]

The first heritage school, Denver Bible Institute, found humble beginnings in the autumn of 1914. The account of Clifton L. Fowler starting the Denver Bible Institute (DBI) with two students and one teacher in an old plumbing shop tells only part of the story.

Fowler's vision began ten years earlier when in 1904 he confided to Joshua Gravett, pastor of the Galilee Baptist Church, that the Lord had "rolled on him" a vision to start a Bible school in Denver. Fowler soon left Denver to prepare for the challenge: pastoring small churches on the western slope of Colorado and preaching on a horse-circuit; taking classes at William Jewell College (Missouri) and battling the encroaching modernism of the academy; publishing a Bible study magazine

Clifton and Angie Fowler.

Dr. Joshua Gravett:
Long-time Board Member of DBI

Joshua Gravett offered DBI perennial support as it transitioned to new locations and as it broadened its vision to be a liberal arts college, serving on the board of directors for many years. John W. Bradbury writes,

Gravett was one of the most interesting and unusual preachers in the American Protestant pulpit during the first half of the twentieth century. Going to Denver in its early days, staying there as pastor of one congregation for sixty years, he became an "institution" in the "Queen City of the Plains," a veritable patriarch in the Rocky Mountain area! ...He was loved as an evangelist and teacher by churches in nearly half of the states of the union where he held meetings; and many a missionary from the white stretches of Alaska to the steaming jungles of Africa affectionately called him "my pastor."[2]

DBI when it was located at 25th and Welton, 1915.

called *Grace and Truth*[3] for four years and building a network of contributors who held theological viewpoints he admired.[4]

By the time Fowler returned to Denver in 1914 to take over a failed attempt at a school started by Allen Cameron, he had built a solid foundation of experience to mold what would be an enduring, consecrated school that prepares its graduates to change the world.

On the heels of the famous Billy Sunday crusade,[5] Clifton Fowler launched the Denver Bible Institute on September 28, 1914, in a rented storefront near 32nd and Meade Streets and two weeks later started the Sunday Afternoon Bible Class.[6] He set up a curriculum of intensive Bible study and practical Christian work, requiring students to memorize Scripture and develop diagrams and synthesis tools for understanding biblical concepts, and then put their learning into practice. This combination of disciplined learning and immediate practice prepared students to leave the institute ready for ministry.

Eager to build a team of instructors, Fowler recruited Denver pastor and friend Francis W. Starring to share the teaching load. In addition, he drew on the talents of local ministry professionals, including a converted Jewish rabbi who taught a three-week intensive course during that first year.

Within two years, the school had outgrown its facilities. A large home at 25th and Welton was donated to the school. H. A. Sprague '21 described the physical plant for the school from 1916 to 1919:

> The school was housed in one of those old two and one-half story red brick buildings so common during the latter part of the last century which had by care and constant attention been well preserved. The stable to the rear of the property…had been converted by a careful remodeling into a very pleasant chapel room. Everything but the chapel was under one roof and to step into that home of the Denver Bible Institute was to find a print shop in the basement; the kitchen, dining room, office, and classrooms on the first floor; with the rest of the building being used as a dormitory. This equipment was of course very limited and inadequate to long meet the needs of a fast growing school, but for a few years the Lord granted that this should bridge the gap until a larger building and fuller equipment should be supplied.[7]

In 1916, tuition was free, and room and board cost $4 weekly.

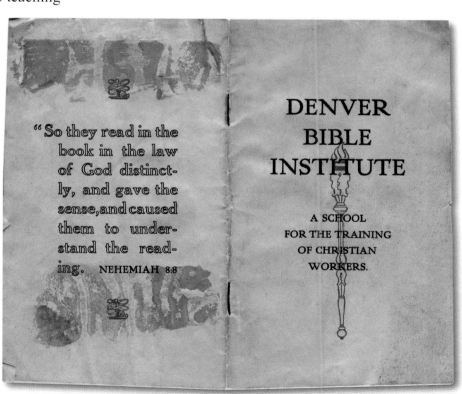

A 1916 DBI brochure.

DBI continued to strain at the seams as the enrollment soared. Students and teachers lived together in increasingly cramped quarters.

DBI students, 1916.

Finally in 1919, the school found what would prove a permanent home: a group of Denver businessmen purchased a large building at 2047 Glenarm Place to house an auditorium, classrooms, a dining hall, and office space. Two buildings nearby were leased as student dormitories. With this move, DBI was incorporated with S. T. McKinney as president and Clifton Fowler as dean.[8]

Students would begin their fall quarter in early October with a day of settling in and registration, followed by a class trip into the mountains for recreation and bonding. The

DBI postcard, circa 1940s.

Eternal Security Dispensationalist

Throughout his years at DBI, Fowler described himself as an eternal security dispensationalist. Scripture that insists Christ died "once for all" (Romans 6:10), that the believer is sanctified "once for all" (Hebrews 10:10), and that believers are "justified from all things" (Acts 13:39) led him to reject the doctrine that a believer may lose his salvation.

Fowler writes, "[B]elievers can truly rejoice for they need not fear. Perfect love (the perfect love of Jesus for His own) has cast out fear. The believer is eternally secure—he shall never be blotted from the Book of Life. Hallelujah, what a Saviour!"[9]

Repeatedly in his classroom teaching and publications, Fowler refers to seven dispensations, or seven time periods characterized by "peculiar method[s] of divine dealing."[10] Together, dispensationalism and the doctrine of eternal security were central to the first two decades of DBI's teaching.

rigorous curriculum kept students focused, and most of the students paid room and board fees through jobs offered to them at DBI.

A fifteen-point statement of faith clearly articulated the conservative theology of the school, and DBI described itself in several advertisements as systematic, interdenominational, efficient, practical, scriptural, inspirational, spiritual, pre-millennial, and evangelistic. This mouthful of adjectives positioned DBI squarely in the Fundamentalist movement, but without ties to a particular denomination.

Without denominational support, DBI was a faith-based institution, one that relied on the ingenuity of the staff and the generosity of supporters. In fact, DBI paid for all expenses on a cash basis, even refusing to accommodate to the practice of paying bills on a thirty-day grace period. Early records are replete with stories of eleventh-hour supply: the donation that perfectly matched the desperately needed funds for Sunday dinner supplies; the pledge for printing equipment paid early, exactly when (unknown to the giver) a bargain machine became available; the offer of a

Students in front of DBI, 1922.

widow to pay the rent on the first classroom building—and sending three of her four children through the institute's program.

One of the most important strengths of the early years of DBI was the network of former students, supporters, alumni, faculty, and staff who, through common bonds and commitment, became a consecrated community. The cumulative effect of this community's connection is astounding. Students of various classes were deeply networked, and they supported one another in their post-DBI careers and families. Even when faculty or administrators left over theological or leadership issues, many continued to rely on one another for Bible conference engagements, employment contacts, and childcare. For instance, Jessie Roy Jones '23 and Florence Jones '27 left their children with Harold and Christine Wilson '18 for several months when they

DBI board member Dr. R. S. Beal and his wife.

An Adventure in Faith

In 1914, Edith Sturgill and Etta B. Stewart ventured to Denver by train and identified themselves to Clifton Fowler by pinning a small square of paper to their coat lapels, joining the only other full-time students at DBI, Dave Brynoff and Forrest Scott. Etta Stewart recalls, "Although it was a very humble place, we were glad to be there. The furnishings consisted of a stove, the teacher's desk, a piano and a number of chairs."[11] Each day, students and the staff would eat breakfast where they lived together nearby the institute and have family devotions with the "lady students" trading off washing dishes so each could have personal quiet time. Students attended classes from 9 a.m. to 1 p.m. and spent a great deal of time memorizing Scripture and serving the community, volunteering at the Sunshine Mission, and visiting recent Jewish immigrants in their homes.

1914–1915 Curriculum
1. Dispensations
2. Analysis
3. Chapter Summary
4. Personal Christian Life
5. Personal Work
6. Bible English
7. Modern Religions

joined the ministry of Carl C. Harwood '37, an evangelist who preached throughout the western United States.

DBI's early mission statement was to "teach the Bible as the Word of God and to train young men and women in the things of the Holy Spirit as they are in Jesus Christ, our Lord." Students at DBI were given responsibilities early and often: they were trained as pressmen and managers of the growing Bible Institute Publishing Company; they ran local missions, including outreach Sunday Schools to underserved areas; they led music ministries; and they held open-air evangelistic meetings around Denver.

Having finished their training, students immediately moved into a wide variety of opportunities, including lifelong service in home missions, Christian education, pastorates, and foreign missions. The first two students who completed the one-year Bible program engaged in a lifetime of national Christian service, Etta B. Stewart '15 as a missionary to Native Americans and Edith Sturgill Lash '15 with her husband in pastorates and at a mission in Pueblo, Colorado.

Harold A. Wilson '18 and his wife Christine Wilson '18 devoted their early careers to pastoring and serving DBI in teaching and administration. Later, Wilson served as the dean of Omaha Bible Institute and as an evangelical leader in Tempe, Arizona. A lifelong contributor to various Christian publications, he concluded his ministry as a pastor in Montana.

Harold Ogilvie '18 and his wife Viola Ogilvie (former student) were the first of scores of DBI students to become foreign missionaries. They joined the Sudan Interior Mission and worked in Nigeria, translating parts of the Old and New Testaments into Iregwe and Hausa and establishing a language school in Jos.

1. Virginia Lieson Brereton, *Training God's Army: The American Bible School, 1880-1940* (Bloomington, IN: Indiana UP, 1990), 128.

2. John W. Bradbury, "Prologue," in *Patriarch of the Rockies: Life Story of Dr. Joshua Gravett* by Margaret Hook Olsen (Golden Bell Press, 1960).

3. *Grace and Truth* (*G&T*) magazine was published by the Bible Institute Publishing Company of Denver Bible Institute. *Western Witness* and the *Rockmont Horizon* were newsletter publications by Western Bible Institute and Rockmont College.

4. Jesse Roy Jones, "The Founder of D.B.I.,"*G&T* (September 1924), 334–6.

5. Famous baseball player-turned-evangelist, "Billy" Sunday opened a revival campaign in Denver on Sunday, September 6, 1914. Reports reached across the U.S. that he had eighty-one participating churches, two hundred volunteers, and a choir of 1,200. "'Billy'

Sunday Attracting Throngs in Denver, Col.," *Pittsburgh Post-Gazette* (September 8, 1914), 21.

6. *Denver Bible Institute: A School for the Training of Christian Workers* (1916 pamphlet), Clifton Fowler Library archive, CCU.

7. H. A. Sprague, "Early Days in D.B.I.: Memories of D.B.I. 21 Years Ago," Special supplement for *G&T* (August 1939), 3.

8. H. A. Wilson, "The Story of D.B.I.," *G&T* (September 1924), 326–330.

9. Clifton Fowler, *The Book of Life* (Denver: Maranatha Press, 1939), 25.

10. Clifton Fowler, *Eighteen Principles of Divine Revelation: A Basic System of Hermeneutics* (Lincoln, Nebraska: Maranatha Press, 1971), 201.

11. Etta B. Stewart, "Early Days in D.B.I.: Memories of the First Year of D.B.I.," *Special Supplement for G&T* (August 1939), 1–2.

CHAPTER 2

Brisk Growth with Strong Connections
1919–1929

The permanent home of the Denver Bible Institute at 2047 Glenarm Place became a springboard for a wide variety of activities that formed the core of DBI's identity. Many young graduates stayed at DBI to pour their lives into the next generation of students; others returned home to serve in vital community ministries. More than half pursued careers in full-time ministry, including a high number committing themselves to a career in foreign missions.

DBI spread its arms to expand avenues of ministry: publishing, Evening School, broadcasting, and Bible conferences. Each one was firmly attached to the growing Day School program.

DBI, 1923.

DBI grew rapidly in the 1920s. S. T. McKinney, pastor of the Fort Worth Congregational Church in Texas, functioned as president, primarily as a remote director. Clifton Fowler was the dean and was involved on site in every aspect of the school. When McKinney resigned in 1924, Fowler did double-duty as president and dean for the next ten years.

The school's doctrinal statement remained firm—DBI was unapologetically evangelical and dependably evangelistic. In the wake of the 1925 Scopes trial,[1] conservative Christian values became suspect in America in a fierce contest with Modernism. While some Christian groups modified their stance to accommodate secular humanism, DBI positioned itself to have a national voice on the side of Christian conservatism.

Graduates and supporters formed what was called the Workers' Group, a dedicated band who performed all tasks, from teaching to financial accounting to kitchen duty. Until the early 1940s, these faculty and staff members worked without pay. At first, the institute provided a small cash allowance of $2 per week for each worker's personal needs, besides providing on-campus room and board.[2] Later, the institute set aside 10 percent of its total receipts and divided the monthly total among the Workers' Group equally—regardless of whether the worker sewed hems or taught Bible classes.

DBI had operated under a no-debt policy until the 1930s. Clifton

Student Life in the 1920s

In 1924, Margaret Beaupre, a third-year student, described student life at DBI: Before breakfast, students straightened their rooms and after breakfast had personal devotional time, which was "often fraught with richest blessing....A time of prayer follows; kneeling there in the morning, before the press of the day's activities...." Afterwards, the girls washed dishes, often while singing a hymn or reciting Bible passages. After a brief chapel service, students divided into various classrooms, and all classes ended by lunch with afternoons free. On Wednesdays, students went out in the late mornings to share the gospel in Denver."

After supper, students had a half-hour prayer meeting. She observes, "[The] keenest of all the testings is that of having the individual life, with its secret hopes and ambitions, its self-satisfaction, transformed by the teachings of God's Word. Things cherished through long years may suddenly appear valueless in the light of some personal teaching; certain habits may be seen as selfish as the searchlight of God's Word is thrown upon them; and what the heart treasured as gold may prove to be dross, when tested by God's standards."[3]

Workers' Group, 1923. *Courtesy of H. A. and Christine Wilson and now part of the CCU archive.*

DBI students and staff.

Fowler notes in a July 1925 editorial in the *Grace and Truth* magazine,

> Following the policy of dependence on the Lord for the supply of each day's need and avoiding all debt, the work has greatly prospered under His hand. Sometimes it has seemed that surely the supply would not arrive in time to meet the need, but not once has this occurred.

Again and again we have begun the day without sufficient funds on hand to purchase food, but we have not yet seen the meal time arrive when there was not full provision for all....To the glory of our Saviour we record that "He is faithful that promised."[4]

By 1927, Fowler's incessant call was "stop that rent drain!" as the school had to lease five buildings to house the ever-increasing student body and staff. The student enrollment fluctuated from fifty to seventy, and the Workers' Group lived on campus as well.

In December 1927, Clifton Fowler talked with the board about relocating west of Denver. In the following months, the board voted its "hearty endorsement of the plan."

Forty acres in Jefferson County. *Courtesy of H. A. and Christine Wilson and now part of the CCU archive.*

Clifton Fowler breaks ground for a new campus, 1928. *Courtesy of H. A. and Christine Wilson and now part of the CCU archive.*

The Spragues and their gospel truck. *From the December 1922 issue of* Grace and Truth *and now part of the CCU archive.*

The Workers' Group and the students gave the same hearty support. In April 1928, Fowler announced an offer of $21,500 was made on a large tract of land in Jefferson County.[5] On July 19, 1928, DBI purchased the land and began building a fresh, useful campus that could accommodate its growing student body.[6]

Graduates in the 1920s

Many of the graduates of DBI during the 1920s were "all in" for Jesus and stayed deeply connected to the DBI family.

Harry Sprague '21 and his wife Selma Sprague '21 invested in a truck, which they named "Emmanuel" and built on its bed a primitive camper. They began travelling to the neglected areas of Colorado in 1923,

sharing the gospel and calling people to renewed faith in Christ. Their gospel truck ministry ended in the mid-1930s because of high fuel costs. They then served neglected home mission fields in central California.[7]

Maurice Dametz '22 pastored small churches on the plains and in local mountain communities and returned to DBI to teach until his retirement. An avid geologist, he led a student club called the "Rock-hounds."

Class president Jesse Roy Jones '23 became the director of music for DBI even

Count Your Many Blessings with Jesse and Florence Jones

Jesse and Florence Jones. *Courtesy of Dave Jones.*

Music Ministry Nets Future Leaders for Christ

The outreach music, preaching, and teaching ministries of DBI were marvelously effective in reaching people in the Denver area for Christ. They also were a valuable recruitment tool. Archie H. Yetter '28 and Betty Burgess Yetter '28 yielded their lives to Christian service through the music and preaching ministries of DBI.

Archie Yetter lived in the neighborhood of the Avoca Valley School, near Denver, in which for several years workers and students from DBI conducted a gospel mission. After some persuasion Mr. Yetter was induced to discontinue the weekly repairs on his "flivver" [Model T Ford automobile] long enough to attend this Sunday-school. Here he was led to trust the Saviour through the ministry of his teacher. Then later, at the close of a service conducted by the DBI male quartet, he gave his life to the Lord for full-time service. The following fall he became a student at the Institute....

Mrs. Yetter, formerly Miss "Betty" Burgess, lived with her parents in Breckenridge, Colorado. Two "Gospel Truck" workers, a man and wife from DBI, were led of the Lord to that little town in the heart of the Rockies. While they were conducting a series of evangelistic services there, the Burgess family took an active part, and "Betty" gave her life to the Lord for Christian work. Later she also entered DBI for training.[8]

Archie and Betty served two years in the Workers' Group. Archie then worked in gold mines, awaiting a call to missions. When China Inland Mission turned down his family for health reasons, he pastored churches in California and Colorado and returned to DBI in 1938 to teach.

In 1954, he was appointed president of Rockmont College, where he served faithfully until 1963 before returning to full-time teaching.

before his graduation, and he stayed on staff for about fifteen years, leading the music department. Along with his wife Florence Jones '27, he traveled widely to lead worship at Bible conferences and in evangelistic ministry. He returned to the school and taught part-time while running a music studio. Florence taught piano at DBI and became a favorite teacher.

C. Reuben Lindquist '27 was Fowler's personal secretary, a faculty member, then dean from 1934 to 1942 and president of DBI from 1937 to 1942. Lindquist hailed from a family of DBI advocates, and two of Lindquist's brothers also attended DBI and continued to work closely with DBI after graduation. Later, Lindquist was the president of the Berean African Missionary Society, which first had been formed as an arm of DBI and then became its own entity in 1937.

Clarence Harwood '28 served as the superintendent of the West Side Center, an outreach to immigrants. With a few colleagues during World War II, he founded the Victory Center for Servicemen and the Spurgeon Memorial Foundation, an evangelistic ministry in Denver. A successful businessman, he was a support to his brother, Carl C. Harwood '37, who founded the Western Bible Institute in 1948.

Evening School

An announcement in the December 1923 *Grace and Truth* offers a glimpse into increasing the accessibility of Bible training in Denver: "On the evening of November 1st [1923] the Denver Bible Institute opened its Evening School. The Institute Evening School offers the opportunity of a conservative study of the Word of God to

The DBI School Song was written by Harold A. Wilson and Clifton L. Fowler and arranged by Mrs. J. R. Jones.
Courtesy of Dave Jones.

Publishing

The Bible Institute Publishing Company launched a premier Bible study magazine in the fall of 1922. This monthly journal supplied intensive biblical exposition and articles on Christian ethics and current events for a distribution that approached 1,500 within the first few months. Clifton Fowler served as editor-in-chief, and senior student L. J. Fowler '23 (no relation) was the business manager.

Linotype machine installed at DBI in 1924.
From the September 1924 issue of Grace and Truth *and now part of the CCU archive.*

employed men and women whose hours of work forbid attendance upon the day school, and opportunity for special training in Bible themes to Sunday School teachers and lay workers of all denominations."

Harold A. Wilson '18 was the superintendent of this school. In his appeal to pastors of the Denver area, Wilson announced the school distinguished itself from the only other nondenominational night school, the Denver Community Training School for Religious Education, by being opposed to the Modernism that has "split the ranks of the believers in the Lord Jesus Christ wide open."[9]

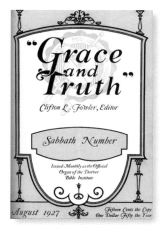

Grace and Truth, 1927.

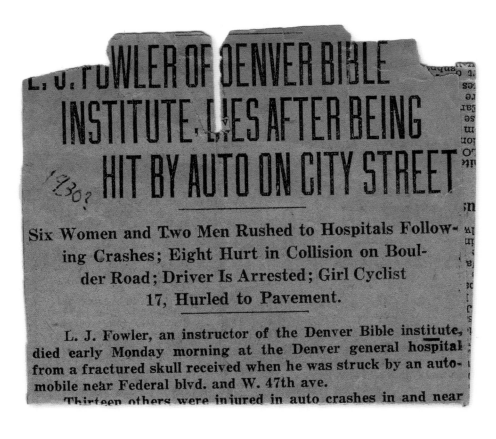

L. J. FOWLER OF DENVER BIBLE INSTITUTE, DIES AFTER BEING HIT BY AUTO ON CITY STREET

Six Women and Two Men Rushed to Hospitals Following Crashes; Eight Hurt in Collision on Boulder Road; Driver Is Arrested; Girl Cyclist 17, Hurled to Pavement.

L. J. Fowler, an instructor of the Denver Bible institute, died early Monday morning at the Denver general hospital from a fractured skull received when he was struck by an automobile near Federal blvd. and W. 47th ave.

Thirteen others were injured in auto crashes in and near

L. J. Fowler dies in a pedestrian accident. *Newspaper and issue unknown.*

In 1927, when L. J. Fowler was tragically killed as a pedestrian in an auto accident, Clifton Fowler lauded the vision of this DBI alumnus:

> I shall recognize him who came to me years ago, standing back of the desk with that peculiar diffidence which I can never forget, offering—I realized with a timidity and restraint that was indescribably deep in his soul—offering the suggestion that I launch the magazine 'Grace and Truth,' as the official organ of the Denver Bible Institute. I shall never, never forget that moment. I said, 'It is a big task, son.' He replied, 'But if you will take the editorial end of the work I will take on the rest of the load.' And he did; with what success, men and women of forty-four states and forty-six countries separate from the United States have testified, telling of the wonderful blessing of God upon the stand and the position and effort made by this child of His.[10]

Institute Park

In the mid-1920s, DBI purchased a 160-acre ranch in Coal Creek Canyon near Pinecliffe, Colorado.[11] At first, the institute used this property for the refreshment of its Workers' Group—a place for summer vacations and retreats. In 1926, one member of the Workers' Group wrote, "At the present time it furnishes an ideal place for the D.B.I. workers, exhausted from a year's toil, to go for recreation and rest in preparation for the coming year of work, and eventually we hope to see it become a summer Bible Conference ground. Its location and natural features make it well fitted for such use."[12] Students, too, enjoyed use of the property and cabins, and many of them spent their honeymoons in the modest "Faith Cottage" on the property.

Outreach Ministries

In February of 1928, Clifton Fowler provided weekly instruction on the International Sunday School Lessons every Saturday evening

Students travel to Institute Park. *Courtesy of H. A. and Christine Wilson and now part of the CCU archive.*

from 8 to 9 p.m. on radio station KOW. The programming soon doubled, with Fowler's Sunday Afternoon Bible Class also being broadcast. Another DBI radio program featured DBI musicians on station KLZ.

DBI held its first Bible conference on February 24–March 1, 1928. The ongoing Bible conferences brought to Denver well-known American Bible teachers for intensive evening and weekend sessions. The Christian Conqueror's Youth Conference was launched in 1939.

Students staffed mission Sunday Schools in rural and underserved areas, working with the American Sunday School Union.

Sacrifice in Service

As DBI graduates began to spread worldwide into the "fields ripe for harvest," they met with thrilling success and sometimes tragedy.

The first missionary death of a former DBI student shook the small DBI community when Ruth Laird, wife of Guy Laird, died of influenza on October 18, 1923, while at a mission outpost near Deri, in French Equatorial Africa. Communication at the time was so poor rumors spread that Ruth had been "clubbed on the head" by natives in an attempt to rescue her, which was inaccurate. Guy Laird continued to minister in French Equatorial Africa. Then, in 1946, Guy contracted sleeping sickness "of the worst type" and he, too, gave his life in service for Christ.

In September of 1937, Irving '36 and Helen Lindquist (former student) were in an auto accident near the Colorado-Nebraska border as they travelled to embark on their mission to the Congo. Irving had recently been the secretary of the Foreign Missions Department of DBI. Helen died nearly immediately and Irving was critically injured. This death especially devastated the DBI community, as Irving's brother was C. Reuben Lindquist '27, president of DBI. Upon recovery, Irving fulfilled his call to serve in the Congo despite this great loss, and after several terms, he returned to DBI in 1943 and married Betty Hess '38. With his new wife, Irving returned to the Congo.

1. The trial of biology teacher John Scopes for breaking Tennessee's anti-evolution law became a national media event. The guilty verdict was overturned a year later.

2. H. A. Wilson, "The Story of D.B.I.," *G&T* (September 1924), 328.

3. Margaret Beaupre, "The Students' Viewpoint," *G&T* (September 1924), 339.

4. Clifton Fowler, "As the Editor Sees It," *G&T* (July 1925), 193.

5. The northwest corner of Colfax and Simms in what is now Lakewood, Colorado.

6. H. A. Wilson, "The Story of the Lord's Dealing," *G&T* (April 1928), 102.

7. Summarized in an entry in *G&T* (December 1923), 42–43.

8. Russell Taft, "In the Harvest Field," *G&T* (August 1931), 268.

9. H. A. Wilson, "As the Editor Sees It," *G&T* (December 1923), 33.

10. Clifton L. Fowler, "Together with Them," *G&T* (April 1927), 101–102.

11. What was DBI's Institute Park is currently Camp Eden owned by Beth Eden Baptist Church, Wheat Ridge, Colorado.

12. Stanley R. Skivington, "D.B.I. at Home and Abroad," *G&T* (August 1926), 247.

CHAPTER 3

Progress and Pressure
1929–1940

Student Life in the 1930s

Students from the 1930s said the most influential aspect of a DBI education was personal spiritual development.

Louise Adams '40 wrote,

Just in case our alarms fail to do their duty, the rising bell is rung at six. Another bell at six-thirty reminds us that before we partake of food for our physical bodies, we need food for our spiritual lives. These quiet times alone with Him prepare us for the day's activities as nothing else can.[1]

R. B. Shoemaker '41 wrote,

After a day of toil and grind, how good it is to again set a few minutes apart and turn our eyes to the Lord. A prayer meeting is scheduled every evening from 6:30 to 7:00. The young ladies meet in the dining hall and the men assemble in the chapel. After a devotional reading, or message, we make known our individual prayer burdens and requests (Phil. 4:5–7).... There is something about these prayer meetings that makes Christ more real to me than in my private room with the Lord. There is something that grips my soul, and causes my heart to cry out to God.... It is my "spiritual filling station."[2]

The 1929 to 1940 era of Denver Bible Institute's story begins with spiritual zeal, energy, and hope—and it ends with echoes of frustration and a determined will to survive. The high quality of graduates during this troubled period are by far the best evidence of DBI's success, for through their fervent devotion to spreading the faith and in their dedication to one another as brothers and sisters in Christ, DBI accomplished its mission.

The new campus in Jefferson County bustled with activity as students and staff themselves built Chapman Hall for classes and meals and began work on Brookes Hall for dormitory space. The $21,500 land purchase price, by far the largest capital outlay DBI had made, was a sample of the demand for several times that amount for new buildings. When funds were slow to come in, Fowler halted progress. Then, when a $200,000 capital campaign failed to materialize needed funds, the school settled for temporary buildings at the cost of $15,000.

Chapman Hall had a classroom and dining facility. *Courtesy of H. A. and Christine Wilson and now part of the CCU archive.*

Students and faculty build Brookes Hall.

Brookes Hall.

Scaffolding on
Brookes Hall.

The farm acreage included in the purchase of DBI's campus provided opportunities for students and staff to produce their own food: garden vegetables, chickens, turkeys, goats, eggs, and milk. Students themselves converted small houses near the campus into temporary dormitory facilities. Several male students even renovated an old chicken house into a dormitory for eight men.[3]

Class of 1935.
*Courtesy of Hazel
Leigh Parcel and
now part of the
CCU archive.*

Class of 1936. *Courtesy of Hazel Leigh Parcel and now part of the CCU archive.*

VALIANT FOR THE TRUTH

REV. CLIFFORD PETERSON

Alumni Banquet, 1937.

Cost of Education at DBI during the Depression

In a letter from C. Reuben Lindquist to incoming freshman Ivan Olsen in 1932, Lindquist outlined the funds Olsen needed for his first year at DBI, 25 percent of which he was required to pay at the outset. Olsen started his four years at DBI with $25 in his pocket, enough to pay the minimum fees for one quarter, and he earned room and board along the way.

Tuition	$50 yearly
Enrollment fee	$4 yearly
Medical fee	$3 yearly
Room and Board	$7 weekly

Beside the entries for books, paper, binders, and ink, Olsen placed dashes—he would have to do without supplies for this first quarter at DBI.[4] A year after Olsen's graduation in September 1937, with the depression lasting much longer than anyone had expected, all tuition was waived.

DBI sign on Colfax. *Courtesy of A. Pauline Teakell and now part of the CCU archive.*

New students arrived every quarter with energy and passion. Alumni, now having crossed the globe with stories of mission work in South America, China, Africa, and the U.S., became the heroes new students admired.

The extension ministries of DBI also experienced a large measure of growth and success. By March of 1939, the Institute Press was operating with newly rebuilt machines, and all production had been relocated from the Glenarm building to the Colfax campus, uniting students and staff in an important way.

Top right: Torrey Hall housed the president and male students.

Middle right: Renovated cottages served as dorms: Broadview #1.

Bottom right: H. J. Smith dormitory. All *courtesy of H. A. and Christine Wilson and now part of the CCU archive.*

Clifton Fowler.

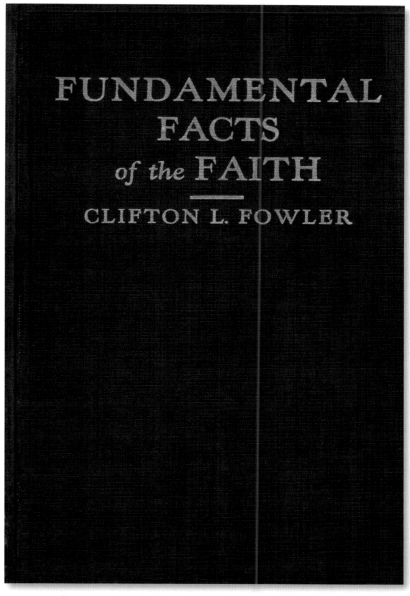

Fowler wrote hundreds of articles, pamphlets, and books.

However, the relentless financial stress of the Great Depression severely dampened the forward-moving vision of DBI. Although student enrollment grew modestly during this decade, since DBI's cost-effective education was attractive, general support did not keep pace with the demand for facilities. DBI for the first time took on debt and mortgaged the Jefferson County campus. On September 2, 1938, foreclosure proceedings against DBI were published in the Jefferson County newspaper. The board put out an urgent appeal to "faithful friends of the Institute" for the $4,000 total needed, and before the foreclosure date of September 26 received the entire amount with an excess of $500.[5]

Perhaps more draining at the time was the domestic and institutional conflict that had been brewing for a decade: Clifton Fowler and Angie Fowler divorced in 1936, drawing suspicion from the conservative constituency. Fowler had an iron in every fire: he was dean until 1933 and president at the time of his divorce; for the Institute Press, he was editor-in-chief and principal writer of pamphlets and books; for Church of the Open Bible (later called the Berean Fundamental Church), he was lead pastor; for the Sunday Afternoon Bible Class, he was lead teacher.

Working Our Way Through DBI

Hazel Leigh (Whitney) Parcel '36 recalls the pace of classes, working, and outreach kept students busy, but not too busy to form relationships that often ended in marriage. She married Leonard Parcel two years after graduation.

For our classes we could use only an unmarked Bible, and *Strong's Concordance*. No study Bibles or commentaries. We had to study it out on our own—then listen to the lectures and take copious notes. We had tough exams every two months. For graduation we must write a thesis of 20,000 words on our choice of Bible subjects.

For 2 years I helped with services in a tiny town, Marshall. Whoever assigned us must have had plans for us, for the 'preacher' I served with was—Leonard....

We even spent quite a number of nights together while we were students—. Well, don't get shocked! It was summer work and the school had much garden and farm produce given to it—far more than we could use immediately—so we canned. It was difficult to do so in the kitchen during days because it was needed for the regular meals—so we worked nights....An auxiliary stove was set up in Brookes' basement and two of us were assigned to work there. Who? You guessed—Leonard and I.

And then we went to Africa together! Well, I was so thankful to be able to work my way—we didn't even pay tuition part of the time.[6]

DBI Men's Quartet, circa 1930s. *Courtesy of Hazel Leigh Parcel and now part of the CCU archive.*

The
Denver Bible Institute

(Incorporated)

Denver, Colorado

Continental Divide

The Bible Training Center
of the
Rocky Mountain Region

MAIN OFFICE - - - - CAMPUS

W. COLFAX AND DANIELS RD.

DOWNTOWN AUDITORIUM AND OFFICE

2047 GLENARM PLACE

DBI Catalogue.

Fowler stepped back from responsibilities incrementally, and the public position of DBI was that he suffered chronic health issues. Indeed, he did have spinal arthritis and he was a pedestrian in a serious accident in 1939 that left him with a broken hip. In 1933, he resigned as dean, and C. Reuben Lindquist '27 stepped into the role. When Harold Wilson '18 left DBI after a struggle over Fowler's administrative decisions and the treatment of workers' children in the daycare, the Sunday Afternoon Bible Classes were suspended for three years. In 1937, Fowler resigned the presidency. In 1938, he no longer taught his two remaining classes, Personal Christian Life and Book Study. By 1940, he had resigned as editor-in-chief of the *Grace and Truth* magazine, and he severed his relationship with DBI's board of directors.

Within a few months after Fowler's complete separation from the institute he had founded, the *Sunday School Times*, a unifying publication of the Fundamentalist movement, reinstated DBI on its list of approved schools.

During this decade of exuberant hope and devastating disappointment, DBI produced some of its most important graduates—a testimony of God's grace and purpose for the school. DBI also developed an official mission branch, and graduates served the first wave of the Berean African Missionary Society to needy areas in the Congo, planting clinics, schools, and churches. The missionary society grew so steadily that it was incorporated and no longer under DBI by 1937.

The era closed with deepening roots, a history of DBI's success in training Christian workers, and a network of committed

Faculty Families

Family life for DBI workers was tough. Money was scarce and the high calling of dedication to DBI's progress sometimes involved what Dave Jones (b. 1925) called "warped, restrictive policies" enforced by Angie Fowler, Clifton Fowler's wife, who would punish children excessively.

The Jones family moved off campus in 1931 to a farm about a mile away, where the parents were able to nurture their own children. Fellow worker C. Reuben Lindquist bought a pony for them, and they experienced the freedoms of young boys exploring the farm fields and playing pranks. Jones remembers,

> A typical day would include early morning chores (emptying the garbage, cleaning the ashes and clinkers out of the coal stove, bringing in wood and coal), washing up, breakfast, brief devotions… Bible reading, perhaps a song, prayer… then off to school 1½ miles away at Maple Grove Dist. 24, country school. Maple Grove School had about 50 kids, roughly half in the first four grades in one room….On rare occasions [brother] Bill would take our pony Teddy to school, along with a bag of hard corn-on-cobs, and we'd tie him up in the shed in one corner of the school grounds. We always rode bare-back, never had a saddle. Great fun![7]

constituents. Archie Yetter '28, who had returned to teach at DBI, noted the accumulated resources of the institute by 1940—property, ministries, and a strong legacy of students:

> A campus on 40 acres with nine buildings in Jefferson County

DBI hosted Bible conferences. *Courtesy of Hazel Leigh Parcel and now part of the CCU archive.*

An auditorium at 2047 Glenarm Place

Denver Institute Park with two buildings on 160 acres near Pinecliffe, Colorado

Institute Publishing, which grew from one hand-operated press to a fully equipped print shop

   – modern composing tables, a linotype, large paper cutter, a stitcher, a multigraph, an addressograph, and three power driven presses

Grace and Truth: circulation of 3000 to 46 states and 40 foreign countries.

Net Worth: $130,000

Staff: 24 full-time

Cumulative enrollment in Day School, 1914-1940: 597 with 127 graduates.

Cumulative enrollment in Evening School, 1914-1940: 264 with 51 graduates.

Total number of graduates, 1914-1940: 178

Total enrollment, 1914-1940: 861 [8]

1. Louise Adams, "Institute Discipline Met My Need…," *G&T* (May 1939), 138.

2. R. B. Shoemaker, "A Spiritual Infilling," *G&T* (May 1939), 141.

3. Dale Jessup, "Denver Bible Institute under the Leadership of Clifton L. Fowler," thesis presented to the University of Denver, July 28, 1959, 111.

4. C. Reuben Lindquist, letter to Ivan Olsen, 1932,

Clifton Fowler Library archive, CCU.

5. Archie Yetter, "Looking Backward," *G&T* (January 1940), 32.

6. Hazel Leigh Parcel, letter to author, Clifton Fowler Library archive, CCU.

7. David Jones, correspondence with author, July 2009.

8. Archie Yetter, "Looking Backward," *G&T* (January 1940), 32.

CHAPTER 4

Rapid Changes
for the DBI Family
1941–1947

After Clifton L. Fowler stepped back from his guidance over DBI in June of 1940, the school remained in the steady, practiced hands of C. Reuben Lindquist '27 who had been president since 1937. Lindquist had been groomed for maintaining the school as Clifton Fowler had formed it—Lindquist had been

Students meet outside Chapman Hall, circa 1940s. *Courtesy of A. Pauline Teakell and now part of the CCU archive.*

Chapman Hall postcard. *Courtesy of A. Pauline Teakell and now part of the CCU archive.*

DBI banner.

DBI student Rose Encinas worked for the Berean African Missionary Society and later married Clifton Fowler. *Courtesy of Hazel Leigh Parcel and now part of the CCU archive.*

Fowler's student, then his personal secretary, then dean. He was a solid fundamentalist and a kind and strong disciplinarian. However, his entire career had been devoted to DBI, and he had little experience dealing

with the rapidly changing shape of Bible schools in America.

The Bible institute culture in America began to shift during and after the WWII era—toward liberal arts education, professional training beyond Bible study, athletics programs, professionally paid staff, and national accreditation. The DBI board and President Lindquist himself had the courage to see some difficult changes were needed.

In May of 1942, Harry A. Davis, the president of the board of the Berean African Missionary Society, died after a long illness. Lindquist had a longstanding investment in the mission as his brother Irving had pioneered missions to the Congo. Lindquist resigned the DBI presidency and took on the leadership of the mission society.

The key speaker for DBI's 1942 summer Bible conference was a Detroit evangelist and nationally known writer and teacher, W. S. Hottel. He needed a home base from which to run his conference teaching; DBI needed national exposure and some

Missionaries Interned— China and Colorado

Mary Fickett Howes '28, a missionary in China, was held by the Japanese for two and one-half years in Shanghai in an internment camp beginning March 3, 1943. She, her husband, and two daughters were interned at the Chapei Civil Assembly Center, which was part of the former campus of the Greater China University. The Howes family shared a room with three other families, a total of thirteen people. Toward the end of the internment, her family survived on several ten-pound Red Cross food parcels that contained the delicacies of Spam, canned butter, and raisins. In her narrative about her experience, Howes quotes lines from a hymn: "When we reach the end of our hoarded resources, Our Father's full giving has only begun." She wrote that "during the period of internment, [God] allowed me to be witness for Him."[1]

Mary Takamine Agatsuma '33 and her family were interned at the Amache Relocation Center near Granada, Colorado, having been moved there from their home near Sacramento, California. The Amache Relocation Center (August 1942 to October 1945) housed 7,597 evacuees, two-thirds of whom were U.S. citizens. Nearly 10 percent of the Amache internees volunteered for military service, and thirty-one sacrificed their lives in the war. Another 120 people died while interned. When first interned, Agatsuma wrote that she looked forward to working as a missionary even in this difficult situation. Her husband, a Methodist minister, coordinated with other groups to aid returnees who returned to California only to find their possessions looted and destroyed.

President Hottel. *From the March 1942 issue of* Grace and Truth.

breathing space from the problems that had smudged its reputation. "It was his sane, practical ministry as the main speaker of the Seventh Annual Summer Bible Conference that led the Board of Directors of the Institute to extend to Mr. Hottel an invitation to serve in the capacity of President," writes the editor of DBI's *Grace and Truth*.[2]

Hottel's administrative speed may have shocked the nearly moribund institute. By October 1942, he was the editor-in-chief of the *Grace and Truth*; he had named a new vice president, John Klein, a local Presbyterian pastor; and he invited new faculty to teach courses in homiletics, practical theology, Vacation Bible School methods, and recreational leadership.

Hottel's vision brought energy as he wisely invited old friends to be new board members: the steady Joshua Gravett of Galilee Baptist Church; Sam Bradford of the growing Beth Eden Baptist Church; Maurice Dametz '22; and Clarence Harwood '28, who was then superintendent of the West Side Center, a ministry to recent immigrants.

Student fun in 1944. *Courtesy of A. Pauline Teakell and now part of the CCU archive.*

These longstanding DBI alumni and friends were necessary because the changes he proposed would have far-reaching consequences. Hottel sought to pay salaries to the faculty and staff, and by 1943 several of the enduring institutions of DBI had to make way for this change. The board voted to discontinue the radio program *Bible Institute of the Air* because it had never been self-supporting and was slotted too late in the evening to have a wide audience. A temporary hiatus on summer Bible conferences "because of the war" relieved the staff from those additional duties.

Student Fun

Before DBI moved back to its Denver campus, students flourished in its rural setting. Anna Pauline Osborn '43 met her husband Claude Fondaw '43 and together they served forty years in Navajo missions. Pauline served another eighteen years after Claude died.

Pauline remembers her DBI days:

I reveled in the Bible teachings of Archie Yetter, Reuben Lindquist and others and thought I was next to heaven. The spiritual atmosphere of the school was unsurpassed.

On the lighter side, I remember the rumor around the school regarding the white shirts the boys were required to wear. There was no casual dressing—always suits and ties....Some of the boys, it seems, had problems with ironing, so they pressed only what would show—the collar, the cuffs, and a strip down the front. When the shirt became spoiled on these three points, it was reversed and became clean, wrong side out.

A situation arose as the boys' and girls' dorms had a clear view across the campus and one couple had figured a system of signals for 9 p.m. They stood in the windows of their lighted rooms facing each other. Soon the faculty reviewed the codes flashing; some students were relocated to rooms on the back side of the dorms.[3]

The largest change was looming. In June of 1943, less than one year into Hottel's presidency, DBI announced it "decided to move the students and classes into the center of the city of Denver where the Institute owns a large debt-free building." The reasons for moving were numerous:

1. Transportation to Denver for mid-week evangelism had become expensive;

2. DBI could better serve Denver churches;

3. Classes would be accessible to Denver commuters;

4. Students would be able to "mingle with the general public";

5. Students could access employment;

6. Students and faculty would have personal conveniences of modern plumbing and an adequate water supply;

7. The move would reduce administrative expenses such as toll calls, gas, maintaining a fleet of vehicles, electricity, maintaining private water systems.

The move required the purchase of more space in Denver, including dormitories. Other buildings were leased to accommodate faculty and staff.

The Berean Fundamental Church, a long-time tenant of DBI's Glenarm Place auditorium, had to find new worship space, and the Berean African Missionary Society (BAMS)[4] moved its headquarters from the Glenarm building to St. Louis. Archie Yetter '28, pastor of the church, and Reuben Lindquist '27, president of the BAMS graciously stepped aside to allow for DBI's progress.

A thorough faculty shake-up was also in the works. Hottel hired Dr. Leo Lapp as dean to guide the academic program, and four new faculty members sported degrees from institutions of higher education. Lapp himself was the first full-time dean who had been prepared in a Bible institute *and* had a liberal arts college degree, which provided the academic legitimacy Hottel desired. Hottel wrote that Lapp had served in the Civil Service and had worked at Bible schools "on a regular salary so that he not

Dr. Leo Lapp.

only knows what Bible Schools teach but also how they are operated."[5]

One can't help but think that such rapid changes in a few short months would offer a promising new start, but that they would also cause an identity crisis. When he moved DBI back to Denver, Hottel announced, "We are looking forward to a real school next term," a statement that combines the promise of positive development with unwise disregard for "dear old DBI's" heritage of rigorous Bible training. Hottel guided these changes from a distance—he continued to run his conference ministry from Detroit and regularly spent time on campus, but not with the sense of "home" known to the committed Workers' Group.

While Hottel was making rapid changes during wartime, a few DBI alumni initiated ministries to serve the military. Clarence

Midnight Bible Institute

Clifton Fowler's outreach continued in his retirement beyond the scope of DBI. During his retirement in Miami, Florida, he mentored young men. Robert V. Finley recounts the Bible teaching he, as a seventeen-year-old runaway, received from Fowler in late-night sessions they enjoyed calling the Midnight Bible Institute: "Fowler would always teach, teach, teach." Finley went on to become a collegiate boxing champion, president of his class at the University of Virginia, an evangelist with Billy Graham and Dawson Trotman, and founder of International Students Inc. and Christian Aid Mission.[6]

Victory Center for Servicemen, 1940s. *Courtesy of the Harwood family and now part of the CCU archive.*

Harwood and Carl Harwood established the Victory Center for Servicemen, recruiting staff from well-trained alumni, including Ralph Obitts '30, a local pastor, and Harold Ogilvie '18, on furlough from Africa. They also launched the Spurgeon Foundation, whose purpose was "the sending of sound Gospel workers into the unreached areas at home and abroad."[7]

The forward progress of DBI continued under Hottel for a second year, and he resigned in 1944, making way for Conservative Baptist leader Sam Bradford to become president. With Hottel's resignation came a 50 percent decrease in faculty: the 1943–1944 school year lists twelve faculty members and the 1944–1945 school year lists six.

President Bradford's church, the Beth Eden Baptist Church at 32nd and Lowell, was rapidly expanding, adding hundreds of members each year. Bradford himself was a denominational leader, serving as president of the Conservative Baptist Association, an arm of the Northern Baptists. He was an entrepreneur in ministry—purchasing the

President Sam Bradford.

Institute Park from DBI for a youth camp, starting Baptist Publications in the basement of his home, coordinating with other ministers in the founding of the Denver Seminary (1950) and Baptist Bible College

☐ **SUSTAINING FELLOWSHIP**
($12.00 a year)

☐ **DAILY NEEDS**
($48.00 a year)

My Contribution To
~~Rockmont College~~
DENVER BIBLE COLLEGE
2011 GLENARM PLACE
DENVER 5, COLORADO

Amount enclosed herewith $................

Name ....

Street ....

City .... State ....

In appreciation for payment in full in advance, or of a payment of $10.00 or more, we will send our magazine "Grace and Truth" for one year, free.

Gift envelope changes.

Music Ministry on the Road

From the early days of DBI, student and faculty music groups took seriously Jesus' command to "Go into all the world and make disciples" and promoted music ministry in churches, Bible conferences, and camps across America. The excerpt below details the 1941 Male Quartet's summer tour:

The student male quartet of the Institute... returned to the Institute on September 15, after an extensive tour of twenty-five states, the District of Columbia, and Canada. In eighty-three days they traveled twelve thousand miles, and held seventy-nine Gospel services. Their ministry in testimony and song was used of the Lord to the salvation of souls and the consecration of lives for Christian service. After hearing the quartet, three young people, one from Illinois and two from Maryland, decided to enter the Institute and are now members of the first-year class....A Christian business man from Chicago wrote, "Our hearts were thrilled at their testimonies and singing."[8]

DBC print shop, 1945.

(1952), and pioneering a radio/television Simacast (1952). While he was president of DBI, his church membership reached over two thousand and the enrollment in Sunday School over one thousand.

Rockmont College on Glenarm Place.

Bookstore.

Bradford's vision for DBI was to be accredited as a Bible college, and he reached this goal within the first year of his presidency. At a meeting on February 9, 1945, the board of directors authorized Bradford and Lapp to apply to the Colorado State Board of Education for a charter for the institute: "All the Directors were deeply conscious of God's dealing and leading, and to them February 9, 1945, marked a great day in the history of our beloved institution, and a step forward into a larger field of service," wrote Maurice Dametz.[9] Less than a month later, on March 6, 1945, DBI received its charter.

In April 1945, Dametz wrote,

We are thrilled as we announce to our readers that the Denver Bible

Institute will open school next fall as a four-year fully accredited Bible college. We have received our charter, and our school will from henceforth be known as DENVER BIBLE COLLEGE. The new college will be the only institution of its kind in the Rocky Mountain area. It will have a course centering around the Bible. It will be possible to take the Bible Institute course and graduate in three years, or continue a fourth year for the college degree.…Although this forward step is being taken in war-time, we are confident that God is going before us.[10]

The school purchased a third building at 2011 Glenarm Place, this one already suited for a college program since it had been the University of Denver School of

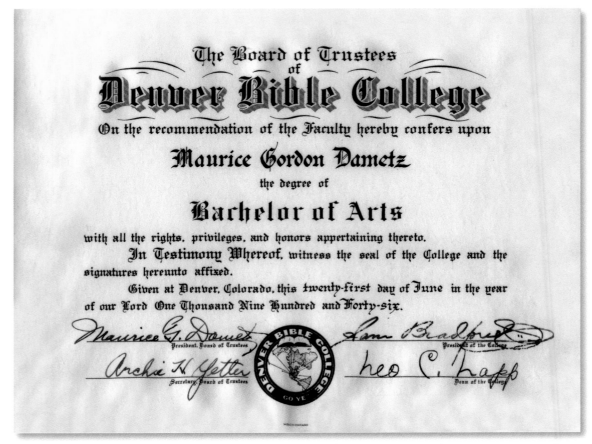

Teacher and student: Maurice Dametz '22 DBI graduates in 1946 with a BA. *Courtesy of Martha Dametz Barhite and now part of the CCU archive.*

Delbert Whitham coached basketball
at DBC.

Commerce. It contained offices, a medical center, "splendid classroom space, and a fine gymnasium."[11] The 2047 Glenarm Place building was converted into more dormitory space, with twelve new double-occupancy rooms, a bathroom, and showers on the second floor.

After the first year of operating as Denver Bible College, the 1946–1947 academic program formally re-organized with three divisions, three deans, and

three degrees. Lapp was dean of theology, offering courses leading to a bachelor degree in theology; Randall Skillen, dean of liberal arts, offering courses leading to bachelor degrees in sociology and Bible; and Archie

DBC advertisement.

DBC pin logo, 1946.

Yetter, dean of the Bible institute, offering courses leading to two-, three-, and four-year Bible diplomas.

The Genesis of Athletics at Denver Bible College

Competitive college athletics became possible for DBI with the purchase of the 2011 Glenarm Place building in 1945, which housed a gymnasium. In April 1946, the board of directors hired Coach Delbert Witham, who also taught history and government.

In the 1947–1948 men's basketball season, DBC achieved an 11-10 winning record. *The Scroll '48* yearbook celebrates the team:

> Our basketball team came through a successful 1947-48 season by winning eleven games out of twenty-one. The season was high-lighted by many closely fought games, evidenced by the fact that twice our team lost by only two points and once by three points. Not only was the team successful in winning a majority of the games played, but under the leadership of Coach Witham, a group of players who had had very little experience at the beginning of the season was developed into a poised, well-trained team. Through all the games a fine Christian testimony was maintained. Our team played hard, it played well, but most important of all it played clean and fair.[12]

1. Mary Fickett Howes, "Experiences in Japan," *G&T* (December 1946), 360–361.

2. C. Reuben Lindquist, "New President of the Denver Bible Institute," *G&T* (September 1942), 310.

3. Pauline Fondaw, Alumni Questionnaire, Clifton Fowler Library archive, CCU.

4. It was the Berean American Mission from 1934 to 1936 and then the Berean African Mission from 1936 to 1937. In October of 1937 it was incorporated as the Berean African Mission Society.

5. W. S. Hottel, "Election of a New Dean," *G&T* (July 1943), 222.

6. Robert Finley, phone interview with author, June 6, 2009.

7. Archie Yetter, "On the Firing Line with the DBI Alumni," *G&T* (November 1944), 342.

8. B. Grace Crooks, "In the Harvest Field," *G&T* (October 1941), 331.

9. Maurice Dametz, "A Great Step Forward," *G&T* (July 1945), 207.

10. Maurice Dametz, "Editorially Speaking: Denver Bible College," *G&T* (April 1945), 102.

11. Special section of *G&T* (September 1945), n.p.

12. *The Scroll '48*, "Basketball," 22.

CHAPTER 5

Two Fresh Schools
1948–1949

The Birth of Western Bible Institute: January 24, 1948

Carl C. Harwood, a man full of passion for Jesus Christ, experimented with new strategies to win people to Christ. By the mid-1940s, he had been a pastor, a traveling evangelist, a trainer for

Carl C. Harwood.

the Child Evangelism Fellowship, and a superintendent of the Victory Center for Servicemen in Denver. He also knew how to have fun and draw others to come alongside him in ministry.

When Harwood's alma mater, DBI, transformed into a Bible college and was on the brink of an even more important transition—to a full-fledged regional liberal arts college—Harwood desired to found a school that focused solely on training students in the Bible.

In the mid-1940s, Harwood was invited to teach an adult Sunday School class at the Overland Gospel Mission at West Evans and South Jason Streets in Denver. On May 30, 1947, he helped form the Western Evangelistic Fellowship (WEF) on that site. The first board minutes declared the group's objective: "It was decided by the group that the purpose shall be to carry on evangelism, missionary work, and all types of Christian work."[1] Harwood started the Practical School of Evangelism through WEF, which opened his eyes to the need for in-depth Bible training. A dream for a Bible school emerged in the fall of 1947.

Carl C. Harwood conducting evangelism on his trick pony MacArthur. *Courtesy of Elsie Fick and now part of the CCU archive.*

An Entrepreneur in Faith

Carl C. Harwood Sr. was a man of great vision and innovation. As a young man, he attended DBI and interrupted his studies to serve as a pastor and evangelist. So effective were his methods for gaining an audience that he soon found an urgent need to train others to satisfy the demand for his services. By the mid-1930s, he was training children's workers in Child Evangelism Fellowship and recruiting students to DBI.

He drew children in rural areas to Vacation Bible Schools through a creative "VBS in a hayloft." He had a trick pony he would use to draw a crowd of fascinated youth to a corral before he taught them from the Bible. In other settings, he used an unusual electronic instrument, a theremin, to draw out the meaning of God's work in our world. A theremin uses electro-magnetic waves to create sound, and the musician "plays" the instrument without touching it. Instead, the musician's body interrupts the waves, creating an eerie range of tones.

At the center for World War II servicemen Harwood and his brother founded, young men stationed in Denver awaiting orders found home-cooked food, a community of caring Christians, and a safe place to socialize. They also heard the gospel.

In November 1948, Harwood advertised a "new scientific demonstration" prepared with rocks and a black light. The phosphorescent rocks glowed a variety of colors, illustrating Harwood's gospel message, another innovative evangelistic method.

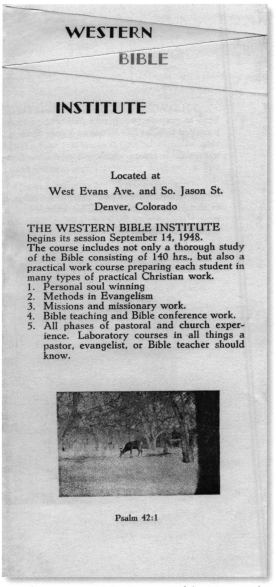

WBI begins in 1948. *Courtesy of the Harwood family and now part of the CCU archive.*

WBI's Purpose Statement

Western Bible Institute exists for a single purpose only, and that is to train yielded Christian young men and women most effectively to give God's Word to a lost and dying world. The School was founded in confidence that the Bible is God's Word and that it is all-sufficient to meet the spiritual needs of souls. Consequently all of its work is shaped in accordance with the conviction that the training which alone is essential for all forms of Christian work is a thorough working knowledge of God's Word. The Western Bible Institute seeks consistently to confine its work to giving this essential training. Every part of the course has been introduced either to impart a clear knowledge of the vital, fundamental teachings of the Bible, to induct the student into a thorough familiarity with the principles which govern all real Bible study, to facilitate his application of those principles in his own study or to assist him clearly and effectively to impart those truths to others.

The Western Bible Institute does not seek primarily to give the student a mass of information about the contents of the Bible, but its first purpose is to train each student to be an independent Bible student, able to dig out the knotty problems of Bible study for himself, and qualified to be of the greatest blessing and help to others in solving their spiritual problems and answering their soul-questions.[2]

Western Bible Institute (WBI) was organized on January 24, 1948, with board members, a clear purpose statement, a school catalog, a dean, and a president—Carl C. Harwood. The Overland Gospel Mission voted unanimously in March 1948 to turn over the deed for the building so the school could expand the physical plant with a surplus war building. WBI functioned in these buildings beginning in 1948 with two teachers and eight students. Within three years, the WBI board was negotiating the purchase of more buildings in its neighborhood and leasing one nearby.

Western Bible Institute, 1948.

"The harvest truly is plenteous, but . . .

WE HAVE A PLAN

← ← ←

the laborers are few."

WBI trains evangelists. *Courtesy of the Harwood family and now part of the CCU archive.*

WBI's first graduate, Carl C. Harwood Jr. '50, the president's son, immediately set his heart on Christian service. WEC's minutes from 1951 read, "How we rejoice to see how the first graduate of the Western Bible Institute, our brother Carl Harwood, Jr., is working for the Lord and how the Lord is certainly blessing in every way and most of all we rejoice to hear that souls are being saved." President Harwood trained his students by taking the entire student body with him as he preached.

WBI faculty took on multiple roles: President Harwood taught evangelism and speech; Archie H. Yetter served as dean and taught the Bible classes; and Elsie Fick first

Miss Elsie Fick

Elsie Fick was on the original board of WBI, an unusual position for a woman of her era, and she taught and served in the school for decades. She was among the first to take classes at WBI and was its last graduate, as WBC honored her with a doctorate before it merged with Rockmont.

The daughter of a blacksmith in Central City, Colorado, Elsie grew up in a Christian home and attended so many conferences, revivals, and evangelistic meetings that she did not remember the date of her conversion to Christ. She had one desire for her life: to attend a Bible institute. But an aunt intervened, and Elsie became a teacher after graduating from the University of Denver.

After ten years of teaching, she partnered with Carl C. Harwood as a pianist in his evangelism ministry and was later a student at WBI, working in the print shop. After graduation, she served as registrar and taught English, speech, and Bible courses.

She was known for her personal interest in students and kept a wall of pictures beside her desk that reminded her to pray for each individual. Dave Bober WBI '70–'71 paid tribute to her:

My favorite teacher was Miss Elsie Fick. She was a tough, no-nonsense kind of teacher but always brought the best out of her students. When I entered her English class in the fall of '70, she realized that I was extremely shy—almost a recluse. But she wouldn't let me stay that way…. I remember my first oral book report—I had it memorized word for word but was still petrified and wanted to run out of the class door. But Miss Elsie blocked the doorway and said, "I'll help you." And she did! I have often thanked the Lord for her faithfulness, genuine concern, and ability to motivate.[3]

Elsie Fick's class.

taught child evangelism classes and later taught Bible and English classes. With a certain "family feel," the board members included Mildred Harwood (President Harwood's wife), William A. Fick and Helen Fick (Elsie's father and sister), and other long-time friends. The board sought "to take just a few students and train them well." Because several board members were also involved with Denver Bible College or were alumni of DBI, the board stated frankly that "the purpose of the school is to be constructive and not to conflict with the teaching or work of other schools."[4]

Elsie Fick's prayer board.

A Transformation: Denver Bible College to Rockmont College, 1948–1949

Denver Bible College experienced the blessing of an overflowing student enrollment partly because of President Bradford's influential Baptist ministry at Beth Eden Baptist Church and partly because of the 1944 GI Bill, which supported higher education for veterans. Bradford and his administration believed the label "Denver Bible College" limited the school; he desired a regional and wider influence. He proposed "Rockmont College" as the new name for "dear old DBI." The name drew on the Rocky Mountain region and echoed a program that Bradford admired, Westmont College in Santa Barbara, California.

John Wood, a student editor of *The Student Voice*, wrote,

Rockmont College is the third step in the growth of an institution originally founded in 1914 as Denver Bible Institute. The Institute later became the Denver Bible College, which was an institute on collegiate level. Because of the growing demand among conservative Christians for a Christian liberal arts college, the Rockmont College program was set up.

The Christian theistic philosophy, which is the basis for our plan, begins with the theory held by our conservative Christian clientele that the Bible is the record of God's revelation to man. We believe that the whole universe is the natural revelation of God, revealing His power and presence at every point, while the Bible is His special revelation, revealing His persona and purpose in Jesus Christ.[5]

The First Yearbook

The first DBC yearbook, *The Scroll*, was published in 1948. It featured fourteen seniors, three students in the School of Theology, twenty-three juniors, fifty-three sophomores, and fifty-one freshmen, a total of 144 students.

At the time, DBC had four music groups: the DBC Chorus, the King's Harmoneers (male quartet), the Girls' Trio, and the King's Four (a mixed quartet). DBC boasted a camera club led by Archie Yetter and a basketball team coached by Delbert Witham.

The
SCROLL

1948

Published by
The Students of Denver Bible College
Denver, Colo.

Rockmont's first yearbook.

Merry Christmas

The Student Voice

Vol. 2, No. 3

Published Monthly by
ROCKMONT COLLEGE, DENVER, COLORADO

December, 1948

Kangaroo Court Convenes

by Robert Connerly

Kangaroo Court for the violators of Rockmont's Code of Laws for Freshmen met for its first session November 24th.

Most flagrant of the violations among the freshmen which caused the court to convene, were failure to keep rocks in possession at all times; using stairway reserved for upper classmen only, and failure to greet upper classmen with a smile upon meeting or passing.

Dick "200 Watt" Mattson and Tom "Level Head" Graham acted as Judge and Bailiff of the court. The prosecuting attorney was Herb Dinsmore and the attorney for the defense, Roland Dahlberg. The jury was composed of Cliff Morton, Ray Noland, Keith Fredrickson, Dean Skillen, Mrs Sullivan and Dr. Fuhrman.

The Bailiff swore in the accused with the customary dignity. "Raise your right leg. Do you promise to tell the truth, the whole truth, and anything but the truth, so help you Skillen?"

After all accused freshmen were

Mountain Roll-Call

by Roland Dahlberg

"Hey Mr. Lapp, is this a fish?" "Where's Mr. Conard?", "Is this rock igneous or sedimentary?", "Boy, am I hungry, when do we eat?" These and similar questions were heard during the geological field trip that the

Dr. Oswald J. Smith to Speak at Homecoming

by Cliff Morton

Dr. Oswald J. Smith of the Peoples Church, Toronto, Canada, and Rev. I. Cedric Peterson, General Director of the Conservative Baptist Association of America, will be guest speakers at Rockmont's first annual homecoming, January 12 through January 14, 1949.

C. U. Loans PsychiatricDisplay To Rockmont

by William Busby

"Sixty-five percent of all mentally ill persons can make a complete recovery, and return to normal social activities if given a chance." This is the essence of a lecture that was given by Dr. R. Robert Cohen of the University of Colorado School of Medicine, Tuesday night, November 30, at Rockmont College. The lectures were repeated on Thursday night, December 2.

Dr. Cohen made it clear that there is no such thing as a "crazy" person, and that one with mental illness is no more "unlucky" than one with any physical maladjustment. "Any behavior, normal or abnormal, is an attempt of the personality to conform to its surroundings," stated Dr. Cohen.

The discussion was accompanied by visual demonstrations indicating the various aspects explained by the psychintrist. These were presented in a series of booths set up in the student lounge of the college, for the purpose.

The speaker stressed the need for education of parents in a developmental procedure for children of very

Dr. Smith's church supports over two hundred fifty missionaries and last year gave $145,000 toward the carrying out of Christ's Great Commission. It is said that people who want a seat in his church on Sunday morning must arrive there before 7 a. m., and if an entrance into that building is to be gained, it must be before 9 a. m.

Rev. Peterson comes from Chicago, where for 12 years he has been pastor of the Lorimer Memorial Baptist Church. When Rev. Peterson was first called there, he found the church surrounded by a foreign population, so he went out two miles and established a new work. Since that time, both churches have grown and now a new work is being carried on two miles farther away. Rev. Peterson was the first treasurer for the C.B.F.M.S., and is a great leader among conservative Christians.

PROGRAM
Wednesday, January 12
10:45 a. m. - 11:10 a. m.—college chapel
Rev. I. Cedric Peterson
Dr. Oswald J. Smith
2 p. m.—college chapel
Dr. Oswald Smith
(for preachers)
7:30 p. m.
Dr. Oswald Smith
(for public of Denver)
Thursday, January 13
10:45 a. m. - 11:10 a. m.—college chapel
Rev. I. Cedric Peterson
2 p. m.
Dr. Oswald J. Smith
Rev. I. Cedric Peterson

Rockmont College newspaper, 1948.

Seeking ongoing accreditation with the newly formed Accrediting Association of Bible Institutes and Bible Colleges, Rockmont required of each student thirty credit hours of Bible coursework. The liberal arts program was built around this foundation.

What did a four-year plan look like for the typical Rockmont student? Biblical studies and worldview classes, along with English and communications formed the first year. Second-year students studied social sciences, literature, and science,

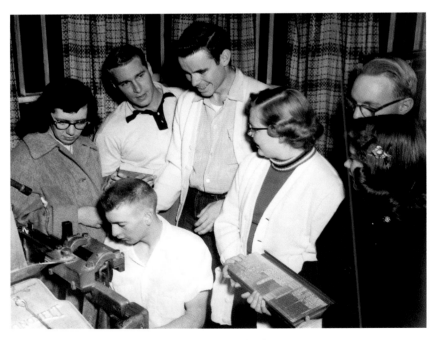

Students learn the craft of printing.

ROCKMONT COLLEGE

DENVER, COLORADO

Presents

THE KING'S MESSENGERS

IN A PROGRAM OF

GOSPEL MUSIC

TIME_____

PLACE_____

The King's Messengers.

along with Bible courses. Third-year students declared their majors and began language and vocational courses along with natural sciences. Finally, senior students took electives in their majors and studied Christian doctrine.

From 1948 to 1949, the Bible institute division of Rockmont dissolved, opening the way for Archie Yetter to apply his gifts with Harwood's efforts in starting Western Bible Institute. Rockmont's theology division was absorbed into the liberal arts curriculum. At the same time, W. Randall

Skillen Jr., who had been hired in 1946 as an instructor in Christian education, was quickly promoted through the ranks: from instructor (1946 to 1947) to dean of liberal arts (1947 to 1948) to dean of Rockmont (1948 to 1949) to executive vice president (1949 to 1950).

What effect did the fresh and potentially large changes have on students? According to Tom Graham '50 and Dougal Graham '50, not much. Tom Graham noted students were concerned about accreditation. He also joked that when Rockmont students were asked their major, they would say, "I'm majoring in Leo Lapp," a popular Bible and theology professor. Dougal Graham said he had come to DBC because of a chapel message by W. S. Hottel, whose instruction Graham said "grips you and pulls you into the grace of God."[6] But he found continued strong Bible teaching and theology training under Lapp and Thomas Murray after President Hottel resigned.

As a Bible college and then as a liberal arts college, Rockmont continued to train students for Christian service. The 1950 *Signet*, the college yearbook, shows the seniors planned careers as pastors, missionaries, educators, and youth workers. Mission Prayer Bands, the Embryonic Preachers' Club, and the Soul Winners' Club continued to draw enthusiastic students alongside the Click-in Time Club (photography) and the Rockhounds (geology/paleontology). Christian service in the form of fieldwork dominated many students' weekends, as they ministered in neglected areas around Denver and in mountain Sunday Schools.

1. Minutes of the Western Evangelistic Fellowship, May 30, 1947, Clifton Fowler Library archive, CCU.

2. Carl C. Harwood, capital campaign poster by G. F. Gemeroy, n.d., Clifton Fowler Library archive, CCU.

3. Dave Bober, Alumni Questionnaire, Clifton Fowler Library archive, CCU.

4. Minutes of the Western Evangelistic Fellowship, January 24, 1948, Clifton Fowler Library archive, CCU.

5. John Wood, "Rockmont Pioneers in Christian Education," *The Student Voice* (October 1948), 3.

6. Dougal Graham and Thomas Graham, interview with author, August 4, 2009.

CHAPTER 6

Teaching the Word, Reaching the World
1950–1963

Western Bible Institute

By March 1951, WBI's vision for training young men and women in Christian ministry was blossoming. The board appointed Helen Fick, Elsie's sister, to begin the process of accreditation with the American Association of Bible Colleges, and President Harwood sought to secure the home of WBI by transferring to the school the deed from the Western Evangelistic Center. In addition, the school purchased adjacent land for future expansion.[1]

Dean Archie Yetter, who was on the original board that had formed WBI, resigned his position to follow other avenues of ministry in 1952. He would soon return to his teaching post at Rockmont, keeping the relationship between these two schools alive. Harwood took on the role of dean of

Western Bible Institute Catalog, circa 1960. *Courtesy of the Harwood family and now part of the CCU archive.*

Bible Trivia Contest. *Courtesy of the Harwood family and now part of the CCU archive.*

WBI in addition to being president. Carl C. Harwood Jr. assisted the school in teaching and administrative duties alongside his pastorate at Central Bible Church, becoming vice president of WBI in 1953.

A high level of sacrifice among the faculty and administrators of the school set the pace for growth. As the school graduated its first class of night school candidates in 1953 and doubled the budget from just over $7,000 to more than $14,000 in 1954, the salaries for administrators and faculty decreased. Where were the funds spent? On a new student dormitory.

President Harwood had proved himself a creative ministry leader, and the new financial challenges sparked in him inventive plans for acquiring the funds needed for the growing school. At least one of the fundraising attempts was contentious; a Bible trivia contest was construed as gambling. Subscribers paid a $2 entrance fee, and winners won substantial cash prizes. A poster-sized ad ran nationally and doubled as a marketing strategy to communicate the opportunities at WBI. This fundraising campaign caused significant unrest among the board. Part of the problem was the high financial risk—initial fees and expenses were nearly $30,000, double WBI's

Innovative Fundraising at WBI

How many Bible schools can boast about a western cattle round up as part of its operations? One of several projects that proved successful in fundraising for WBI was running a small cattle operation on land loaned to the school. Beginning in the early 1950s, funds were set aside for the purchase of cattle, feed, and supplies. The proceeds from the operation circulated back into the school, providing seed money for more fundraising activities. Cattle operations, with expenses of about $2,000–$3,000, netted an income of about $500. A farm leased in Idaho and worked by a friend of WBI produced beets; various initiatives netted the school tens of thousands of dollars, several times the annual budget.

annual budget. Some questioned the legality and ethics of interstate gambling. In the end, the contest netted a large positive return to the school, was repeated for one more round, and then discontinued.

Because WBI was mission-minded and evangelism-driven, the school yearned to train international students who would return to their nations as evangelists. During the 1950s, President Harwood and his son flew to Fiji to secure contacts and recruit students, part of a concerted effort to widen the scope of WBI's influence. International students often paid little or no tuition. In the spring of 1962, graduates began returning home to minister to their own nations; two students returned to the British West Indies and one to Fiji. Joseph Lulich '63 began an evangelistic ministry at home in Italy. WBI also hosted students from South Rhodesia, the Congo, Pakistan, Singapore, and Jamaica.

By the winter of 1956 to 1957, all of WBI's property was listed for sale—not because of financial difficulty but because the dream for the institute's growth required a campus move. Zoning at the Jason Street property prohibited any further expansion, and the facilities were crowded. Most of the available space was used for housing, and classes were held on the third floor of the First Christian Church in Englewood.

President Harwood did not live to see the next phase of WBI's progress, as he died of complications with diabetes in 1957. His evangelism training secured WBI's reputation and his creative fundraising secured its future. In the same year of his death, the final funds for the Bible puzzle contest were deposited, and all of WBI's debts and loans were repaid in full. Although not yet liquid, the assets of the school exceeded $200,000 before its tenth anniversary. Carl C. Harwood Jr. became the second WBI president.

Carl C. Harwood Jr. *Courtesy of Elsie Fick and now part of the CCU archive.*

In October 1958, Clarence R. Harwood (the late Carl Harwood Sr.'s brother) and Stan Harwood (Clarence's son) joined the board of WBI. Clarence was a 1928 graduate of DBI and a long-time board member there. Clarence and Stan, owners of the profitable Purity Creamery, committed their time and business profits to ministry. In 1959, WBI board minutes record this information: "A motion was made by Clyde Shaffstall and seconded by Mildred Harwood that we accept with humble gratitude the property offered to the Western Bible Institute for a campus. Said property is located in Jefferson County. Motion carried."[2] The "said property" was a gift from the Harwood family, prime real estate already platted into forty lots, valued then at $140,000.

On the same day the board of WBI accepted the Harwood gift, all gears went into motion to build a new campus. Letters were sent to the Denver office of the U.S. Department of Health, Education, and Welfare to purchase surplus buildings from Lowry Air Force Base at a significant discount. A budget for moving, remodeling, and installing the buildings was detailed. A plan for the installation of the buildings and the use of the buildings for educational purposes was provided to the government office.

Loans were secured from Purity Creamery and First National Bank to complete the campus. Twenty-three buildings, all formerly dwellings, were moved to the new property. The cost of the buildings was low—a total of $2,850—

WBI campus in 1961. *Courtesy of the Harwood family and now part of the CCU archive.*

but building a campus strained the purse strings—over $88,000. Even the Harwood children and grandchildren helped prepare the buildings for students by working on drywall. However, the drive for a new campus did not distract WBI from its central focus. The school had a standing policy of tithing 10 percent of all income to mission opportunities, and even in this trying time, a full tithe was paid out. By fall 1960, the dream of a new campus had become a reality, and students moved over Christmas break 1960–1961.

The mission of WBI was to teach the Bible and to reach the world:

> The Western Bible Institute exists for the single purpose of training yielded Christian young men and women most effectively to give God's Word to a lost and dying world. The School was founded in confidence that the Bible is God's Word and that it is all-sufficient to meet the spiritual needs of souls.

> Every part of the Bible Course offered to students by the Institute is introduced either to impart a clear knowledge of the vital teachings of the Bible; to induct the student into a thorough familiarity with the principles which govern Bible study; to facilitate his application of those principles in his own study; or to assist him clearly and effectively to impart those truths to others.[3]

Students had half-day schedules, beginning with a wake-up regimen at 5:30 a.m. and ending with a noon community meal. They paid $4.50 per credit hour and $270 for a semester's room and board. If they needed rides to Denver for jobs, they could arrange for "the school's Cadillac"— one way was 20 cents, round trip 35 cents.

Rockmont College

When Sam Bradford offered his resignation from the presidency of Rockmont in 1950, the school had recently experienced peaking growth. However,

Student Life at WBI and Rockmont

Joy Iden '62 WBI

> The [WBI] dorms were just south of Evans along the Platte River. Every morning we all rode in a big old bus over to where classes were in the education building of the First Christian Church of Englewood. Over Christmas break 1960-1961 the school moved out to Morrison. I was an unchurched—relatively—new Christian when I came to WBI. I had to learn everything about the Bible and the Christian life in those three years to get me established in the Word and my walk with God. It was a good foundation.[4]

Nova Felkins Bailey '51 Rockmont

> [I remember] the singing in the [Rockmont] lounge between dinner and study hours; and before the blessing as we gathered in the dining room. Once at the beginning of Christmas break, June Montague was playing "O Come All Ye Faithful" on the piano. Bill Kiery began singing in German, Carmen Manriquez in Spanish, so I sang in Latin. This so confused June that she stopped playing….My Rockmont years were good ones, even as busy as they were.[5]

Student fun.

WBI's Dating Policy in the 1960s

Per the *WBI Student's Guide*:

All students are permitted two dating privileges weekly. These are to be chosen from the following list, and request in each case should be made to the dorm supervisor, except for attendance at church services.

Friday	6:00 p.m.	to	10:30 p.m.
Saturday	1:00 p.m.	to	6:00 p.m.
Saturday	6:00 p.m.	to	10:30 p.m.
Sunday	1:00 p.m.	to	6:00 p.m.
Sunday	6:00 p.m.	to	10:30 p.m.

You may also request a week-night permission, if desired for special occasions.

Meeting of couples outside of designated dating hours are to be on campus, and are to be brief and in good taste at the following times: 5:30-6:00 P.M. or if employment necessitates from 12:30-1:00 P.M....Dating couples may sit together at the evening meal only. No dating couple should be alone in any of the buildings without permission.

...Dating students may travel to and from services and functions outside of their chosen dating occasion(s) provided they do not sit together in the conveyance or at the function.

a sharp decline in student enrollment soon followed. After a high of more than 230 students at the end of the 1940s, the 1953 enrollment hovered at the mid-150 range. Rockmont had benefited strongly from Bradford's connection with Beth Eden Baptist Church and from the GI Bill, which funded the education of recent veterans. Bradford's departure, along with the loss of the postwar flood of students, resulted in strained finances. As Bradford moved into a more narrow fundamentalist direction, his split from Rockmont became even more clearly defined. In 1952, Bradford founded his own Baptist Bible college in the Beth Eden Baptist Church facilities, which competed for the same students and support base.

Dr. W. Randall Skillen Jr., who had been a faculty member, dean, and executive vice president under Bradford, was elected the new president of Rockmont in 1950. Lewis Price, one of Skillen's students, remembers him as one highly skilled in listening, questioning, and expanding students' worldview. Price considered his own spiritual development under Skillen's leadership a "second conversion," one that integrated biblical knowledge with the liberal arts.[6] The young Skillen family enjoyed the extracurricular activities of students, opening their home for the yearly crazy Halloween parties and accompanying students on music tours. Once, students pranked their president by installing an outhouse on his front yard.

President Skillen.

Skillen led the school during a season of turmoil caused by the financial pressures of declining enrollment and a struggle over Rockmont's move into liberal arts education. The idea of a Christian liberal arts college, given Rockmont's history as a Bible institute, caused confusion among alumni and donors. Skillen tried to compensate for the financial stress by reducing faculty to a part-time basis and leading Rockmont more strongly in the direction of liberal arts from a Christian worldview. The inequity in pay and the lack of buy-in by alumni and supporters culminated in the resignation of Skillen and

President Archie Yetter.

the January 1954 appointment of Archie H. Yetter as acting president.

For practical reasons, Yetter was an ideal candidate to lead Rockmont: he was a 1928 alumnus of DBI, he had built a fine reputation as a Bible teacher, he was known as a man

Dr. Archie Yetter: Inspiration for Service

Eldon Wilford Coffey '50 remembers Archie Yetter's quiet but strong challenge: "One day at Camp Id Ra Ha Je, Pastor Yetter & I were lying on the grass discussing life in general. He made this statement I never forgot: 'Eldon it looks like it's up to you & me to carry on this spiritual work for God's glory.'" Coffey served Christ for a lifetime, as pastor of three churches, as a Veterans Administration chaplain, and as a minister to seniors.[7]

Bill Barlow '56 wrote, "Dr. Yetter led the college when it moved to Longmont. His character, scholarship, and teaching were beacons to staff and students alike, including Dr. Beckman." Barlow went on to earn an MA from the University of Colorado and serve as an administrator in Christian schools as a pastor and as a minister under Prison Fellowship and Set Free Prison Ministries.[8]

Rockmont College Choir.

Rockmont Band.

Rockmont Girl's Trio, 1951.

of integrity among churches he pastored in metro-Denver, and with his wife's inheritance he had the ability to support himself financially, however meagerly.

In the early 1950s, student activities included a strong music program, with choirs led by Aram Philibosian, annual performances of *The Messiah* and *Elijah*, and instrumental groups such as a band and a brass quartet led by Jesse Roy Jones. The athletics program and activities included a men's basketball team complete with cheerleaders.

Yetter took on the presidency at the forefront of some drastic changes ahead. With its debts, decreasing enrollment, and withdrawing alumni support, Rockmont

LONGMONT COLORADO

WELCOMES YOU

To Live, Work
or Play in

*"The Friendly City
of the Friendly
West."*

Longmont welcomed Rockmont. *Courtesy of the Longmont Chamber of Commerce and now part of the CCU archive.*

Rockmont College in the old Bryant School.

Rockmont students, 1954. *Courtesy of Mary Yetter Crotts and now part of the CCU archive.*

needed to sell its property and find a less expensive "home." After some exploration of properties on Santa Fe south of Denver, the administration was surprised by the City of Longmont's generous welcome, and Rockmont moved north of the Denver metro area. Rockmont opened its doors in Longmont in the fall of 1954 in the abandoned Bryant School for classrooms, rented space in homes and nearby apartments for dormitories, and a dining hall in President Yetter's basement.

Rockmont women's dorm.

The academic program was streamlined: students could choose among music, education, religion, and general

Studying.

The Greek Club, Rockmont College.

Rockmont flag raising.

education studies. The men's basketball team, "The Rockets," survived and competed in a community gymnasium, and the music program continued under the new direction of Gaylord Taylor.

Some professors followed Rockmont northward—including Maurice Dametz and the Joneses. Others found the commute or the low pay too difficult. By the late 1950s, only a handful of professors remained, and among them a new favorite, Donald Kopecky '50, who would teach Bible and Greek for many years and serve as dean of students and dean of faculty. The support staff was a

"family affair," with Betty Yetter '28 as cook, Elaine Kopecky '48 as secretary to the president, and students as office workers and caretakers.

How was this small school to thrive? Yetter led the school toward a vision of a new campus on Collyer Street about a mile north of Longmont. The 1957 Rockmont yearbook, the *Signet*, opens to an inside cover that lays out plans for the new campus. This design phase contains sketches of dormitories, classrooms, a gym, an auditorium, an observation tower, athletic fields, and a president's home. Two years later, the 1958–1959 *Signet* shows

Aviation Studies at Rockmont

Rockmont had an aviation club for students as early as 1947. The Flight Club, a formal program in aviation training, started in 1951, led by Dr. Marian Fuhrman, who was the dean of women and a Greek and sociology professor.

When Rockmont moved to Longmont in 1954, supporters banded together to keep the program going for more than a decade. In September 1963, the *Rockmont Horizon*, an alumni newsletter, states:

Did you know...that during the school year of 1962-63, Rockmont College acquired a Cessna 140 aircraft so that the flight major might be more fully implemented?

...that two Christian pilots, Hugh Chance, a Captain with United Airlines, and the man who founded the flight major, and Bob Matthews, a graduate of the Moody Bible Institute's Missionary Aviation program, are giving time, effort, and financial support to Rockmont's flight major?

Longmont building site for Rockmont. *Courtesy of the Longmont Chamber of Commerce and now part of the CCU archive.*

a new day for
ROCKMONT...

Above: Rockmont's new campus in Longmont.

Left: Rockmont looks to a bright future in Longmont.

Below: Rockmont students in Longmont.

pictures of the completed first building, a multi-functional structure with a two-story center hub.

The energy and financial support to build this twenty-five-year campus plan was slow to materialize, and Rockmont struggled to grow. By the early 1960s, people of various talents pitched in to help the school hold on. Dr. E. B. Dickey, a local Longmont dentist and the Rockmont board president, taught health science while alumnus Dougal Graham '50 taught social science. An aviation program started with a donated Cessna 140.

The small number of students set the tone for close community. Many students appreciated the firm Bible foundation they received, and they were inspired for Christian service. Desiring to return to full-time teaching, Yetter worked with the board to find a new president. Dr. L. David Beckman answered the call.

The transition from the presidencies of Yetter to Beckman honored Rockmont's origins. At the last graduation at which he would officiate in 1963, President Yetter helped confer to Clifton L. Fowler, his

Clifton Fowler honored by Rockmont.

teacher and the founder of DBI, the degree of doctor of divinity. In addition, long-time teacher Maurice Dametz '22 received an honorary doctorate. This celebration of the school's heritage marked the beginning of a new era for an institution that had trained students of the Bible for forty-nine years.

---

1. WBI's property at the time was on Jason Street near West Evans in Denver.

2. WBI Board Minutes, October 1, 1959, Clifton Fowler Library archive, CCU.

3. Western Evangelistic Fellowship Board Minutes, January 24, 1948, Clifton Fowler Library archive, CCU.

4. Joy Iden, 2008 Alumni Questionnaire, Clifton Fowler Library archive, CCU.

5. Nova Felkins Bailey, Rockmont Remembrances (a file of alumni memories collected from a survey), 2005, Clifton Fowler Library archive, CCU.

6. Lewis Price, interview with the author, August 21, 2009.

7. Eldon Wilford Coffey, Alumni Survey 2008, Clifton Fowler Library archive, CCU.

8. Bill Barlow, Alumni Survey 2005, Clifton Fowler Library archive, CCU.

CHAPTER 7

New Beginnings
1963–1968

Rockmont

When President Yetter was ready to step back into teaching full time at Rockmont College, a presidential search committee was formed in 1962. Keith Fredrickson '50 suggested Dallas Theological Seminary graduate Dr. L. David Beckman as a candidate. Beckman was at the time the chair of the Bible department at the King's College in Briarcliff, New York.

Although he was not at first interested in the position, Beckman later caught a vision for Rockmont. At his interview, Beckman pitched the design of a Christian college that would offer general education and biblical studies, grounding students in a Christian worldview, while it had reciprocal arrangements with local colleges and universities to teach the majors. While some students did follow through to get their majors from area universities and colleges, this plan never came to full fruition, partly due to the tenuous fiscal position of Rockmont and partly because of Rockmont's Longmont location.

Rockmont Pond.

Footprint of Rockmont at Garrison and Alameda.

On October 17, 1963, L. David Beckman was inaugurated as president of Rockmont College. When Beckman joined the Rockmont family, the challenges were nearly overwhelming. Rockmont was in a serious financial condition. Its annual budget was about $51,000, and it owed faculty back salaries of $42,000. Moreover, a $200,000 bond issue was due in four years. The class sizes were small. Four students comprised the Senior Class of '64, and each member served as an officer in the class—with no competition.

President L. David Beckman.

Dr. L. David Beckman's Message to the Alumni

September 1963

As we face the responsibilities at Rockmont, we envision two major purposes for the college....As a Christian College, Rockmont is committed to the principle that educated men and women bring big returns for Christ. This, then, is our first purpose: to educate, but to do so within the Christian perspective....

The second major purpose we envision for Rockmont goes beyond that expressed by Mr. Eban [an Israeli diplomat and scholar]. Education alone, though great in its returns, can never be the ultimate answer, either for Israel, or for the work of God. For us, the greatest returns are not found in educational achievement only.

It is only as our students develop a spiritual virility that shall make them active and dynamic witnesses for the living Christ that we shall succeed in giving them the education we desire to give them at Rockmont.[1]

Capital campaign for new campus.

Soon, a vision for a new campus back in the Denver metro area caught hold, and under Beckman's leadership in 1966, Rockmont purchased forty-three acres in Lakewood for $320,000. Funds were raised through a new bond issue that paid off the previous debt and included some costs associated with the new property.

In the fall of 1967, Rockmont's move back to Lakewood brought it within a few short miles of where its predecessor DBI had built its 1928 campus in Jefferson County. Rockmont opened its new campus with excitement and growth. The 1966–1967 enrollment at the Longmont campus had been 107, which increased to 129 in 1967–1968 at the Lakewood campus.

In a letter to the Lakewood community, Dr. Beckman described Rockmont: "Two-thirds of the students are from Colorado, and the other third come from 15 other states and two foreign countries." He stated the administration building and dining hall had been the Howard Reynolds home (later called the Beckman Center). The women's residence building had been the residence of Mrs. Luke Smith only two months earlier (later called the Welcome Center). The men were housed in a duplex at 123-125 Cody Court.[2]

Women's dorm (later the Welcome Center).

Competitive athletics continued as part of Rockmont's program. The head soccer coach made temporary arrangements for athletic activities, such as makeshift soccer goals erected on the northeast practice field.

The move to the new campus was accompanied by rapid development. A dining hall was finished in December, which years later became part of Clifton Fowler Library.

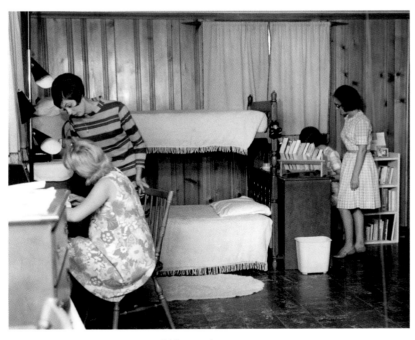

Women's room.

Western Bible Institute

"New beginnings" were also underway for WBI when it announced that 1963–1964 was the first academic year in which a student could earn a bachelor of arts degree in Bible. Two students earned bachelor degrees that year. Minors included sacred music, missions, Christian education, and pastoral ministry. Students could also achieve a three-year Bible certificate.

With the resignation of President Carl C. Harwood Jr. in 1965, WBI entered a time of transition. Harwood continued to pastor Central Bible Church and was the director of General Douglas MacArthur Boys Center in Denver. Faculty member Ronald Merryman took the role as acting president, which lasted nearly three years.

Although the move to the Morrison campus had surged new life and vision in WBI, by 1965 the school was in a financially precarious position. Only a few faculty members were full time, and the board began talking with Rockmont about a merger. President Merryman met often with Rockmont's academic dean, and they hammered out details toward Bible, missions, and Christian education degrees. However, when the conversation turned to a broader liberal arts program, Merryman questioned whether the co-joined school could fund the necessary faculty and library. He also did not agree with Beckman that an alliance with local colleges and universities would result in students gaining a Christian worldview.[3] Rockmont's faculty voted against pursuing a merger at that time.

Merryman confronted WBI's financial problems by bringing on Bob Benson, a former student with business acumen, to help with new financial management, and the faculty pulled together to expand the school's outreach. Together, the board and administration raised $150,000 the first year to renovate the buildings

WBI Acting Presidents Merryman and Wright.

WBI buildings.

with board and batten to make them fit the look of the mountain setting.

Although WBI stayed focused on Bible training, new courses were staffed in 1967–1968, including science courses and linguistics. WBI expanded its teaching to include tuition-free evening classes at sites in Denver. Under Merryman's leadership,

WBI office with Elsie Fick and Carl Harwood Jr. The two men on the right are unidentified. *Courtesy of the Harwood family and now part of the CCU archive.*

WBI adopted a revised statement of faith and refocused the curriculum to be squarely a Bible institute first and a college second.

In 1967, WBI introduced a new curricular department. Christian Education was headed up by a fresh faculty member, Bill Boyd, who with Elsie Fick would be among the longest-serving professors in the school.

Another new beginning for WBI occurred in 1968—the appointment of Dr. Stanley L. Toussaint as the fourth president of the institute. Merryman remained on staff as a professor. The faculty reaffirmed its goal "to prepare Christian students to become lay or full-time witnesses and workers of Christ and His church, witnesses which will effectively and fruitfully serve God and man."[4] The faculty and staff spent their 1968 summer preparing for the new president by compiling reports toward accreditation with the Accrediting Association of Bible Colleges. Toussaint was a well-known Bible teacher at Dallas Theological Seminary since 1960 and his Bible ministry reached around the world. He left WBI after one academic year to take a pastorate in Richmond, Virginia, but soon ended up back at Dallas Theological Seminary and retired after forty-seven combined years of service in 2012.

The "old spirit" of entrepreneurial support at WBI persisted during these crucial institutional transitions. Leonard Brown, a WBI board member and rancher in Kansas, came up with a plan to put top-quality beef on WBI's dining table for a minimal cost. He solicited donations of weaned calves from other ranchers and engaged a few cattlemen to grow them out and feed them for slaughter, with the hope that WBI students would eat

Birth of KWBI

In 1968, WBI sought permission to construct and operate "a new non-commercial, educational FM broadcast station in Morrison, Colorado."

WBI President Toussaint set the radio's goal of ministry, specifically exposition of the Bible, exposure of WBI's music faculty to the public, and training for students in the technical aspects of radio maintenance, engineering, programming, announcing, and Federal Communications Commission rules.

One year after receiving the license from the FCC to build and operate an FM radio station, WBI hired Gary Herr[5] to be the station manager for KWBI. An orchestrated rendition of "All Hail the Power of Jesus' Name" broke forth on FM 91.1 at 3 p.m., March 27, 1971. Herr and student volunteers kept the programming broadcasting from 3 to 9 p.m. daily.[6]

KWBI was the "good news station" that introduced a Bible verse at the close of each news broadcast every two hours. Its profile was 53 percent Christian music and never back-to-back preaching. KWBI had no commercial advertising and by 1973 was operating seventeen hours each day.

well for a year. Carl C. Harwood Sr.'s entrepreneurial financing of the school lived on as people pitched in to use their skills to support the students.

Finally, one of the most important changes in the ministry of WBI originated in 1968—the school purchased an inexpensive, used, A-frame building, moved it to a site on WBI's property, and launched the FM broadcast station KWBI. By the end of 1968, there were still many bridges to cross, but WBI was given two years to set up radio programming.

Colorado Baptist Junior College

With WBI on the far western outskirts of Denver and Rockmont in the farm fields north of Longmont until 1967, the Denver metro area had been left without a Christian college easily accessible to local students. Huitt Barfoot recognized the need for accessible Christian education and established Colorado Baptist Junior College in 1968.

Huitt Barfoot, founder of Colorado Baptist Junior College. *Courtesy of Huitt Barfoot and now part of the CCU archive.*

On April 12, 1968, the Baptist Press, a news service for Southern Baptist churches, issued this announcement:

An Independent Baptist School started by Southern Baptists is expected to open here in September of 1968 with

classes in the buildings of the First Baptist Church of Westminster.

The school, called the Colorado Baptist Junior College, has no official relationship to the Denver Baptist Association or the Colorado General Baptist Convention, but most of the faculty members and founding fathers are Southern Baptists.

…The school's catalogue lists four purposes for the junior college: "A college with sound Baptist doctrine, a college with a Christian atmosphere, a quality two-year liberal arts program, and a college with qualified Christian faculty."

Serving as president of the school is Huitt Barfoot, a Southern Baptist layman and former public school superintendent and principal, college teacher, supervisor of student teachers and registrar of Central Missouri State College. Barfoot led a group of Baptist pastors and laymen to vote last January to create the college.

Colorado Baptist Junior College (CBJC) began serving the needs of ministry personnel by offering classes in September 1968, from 4 to 10 p.m. Monday through Friday. Associate degrees in science and arts could be completed with ninety-six credit hours of coursework.

The idea of a Christian college had long been on Barfoot's heart. As early as his own college years, he believed Christian college education could be vastly improved. Barfoot attended William Jewell College in Missouri, the same school Clifton Fowler had attended before Fowler founded DBI.

Do It Right

Huitt Barfoot had a vision to found a Christian school that would "do it right." He was born March 12, 1924, and lived in southeast Missouri with nine siblings and his parents, who were cotton farmers. His years at William Jewell College were formative in his dream and drive to begin a new kind of Christian college.

Barfoot, his wife, and young son lived in a trailer behind the gym near another student, Owen Lind. "Well, it wasn't long until we decided we didn't like the way the college was run so we decided *then* and *there* that one day we would start a college and show them how to run it," writes Barfoot.

After graduation, Lind went on to work on a graduate degree in Michigan and Barfoot landed a job in education administration, but they continued to talk about "starting *that* college." The two decided Denver would be an ideal location, so Barfoot moved to the Denver area and got a job in a school district. Barfoot decided to pursue the dream without Lind: "I think I know how a minister feels when he is 'called to preach.' I had the same feeling about Colorado Baptist Jr. College—I just could not let go! Once it was completed and on its way, I began to relax and finally withdrew and spent the rest of my career in education."[7]

In his autobiography, Barfoot writes, "I know with certainty that men are called to preach the Gospel and I am equally sure that I was called to start a Christian college in Denver." Every step of his own experience and training led him to this moment— from his work at Central Missouri State University to his experience as an educator in public schools:

> With that knowledge and background and my calling from God, I went to the State Southern Baptist Office in Denver and met with Dr. Braswell, the director. I wanted him to be the first to know my plans and hopefully get his support…. At the request of some of the ministers he allowed me to make my presentation twice at the monthly meeting of all Southern Baptist ministers in the Denver area. To my surprise, privately, they expressed a lot of support. A few even called me offering their facilities and financial support.

> I felt that I must move on. Soon I had selected a very supportive board of directors and had worked out a plan with Reverend Ernest Waite, minister of a church in Westminster, which wasn't too far from where I worked and lived. His church had an attractive educational building and a nice area for a lounge and library. A lawyer friend of mine filed the legal forms with the state and in the fall of 1968, we opened a two-year college under the name of "Colorado Baptist Junior College." All the instructors were state certified in areas they were teaching. All had bachelor's degrees, some masters and two had earned doctorates. I was serving as president and working at my regular job also.[8]

CBJC operated with a part-time staff, a board of trustees consisting of concerned pastors and laypersons, and borrowed church education facilities. The school had meager beginnings, and its identity was

Rev. Ernie Waite, host pastor for
CBJC and long-time supporter.
Courtesy of Mrs. Waite.

What's New in Athletics? Rockmont and CBJC

The 1965–1966 academic year at Rockmont brought a new competitive sport: touch football. Students competed in an official league, and they played students from Conservative Baptist Theological Seminary (now Denver Seminary) and other colleges. Women's volleyball formed, but the competition was limited to a few intercollegiate games. Soccer and basketball shared the limelight as Don Parkin became the soccer coach at the Lakewood campus. Dave Lambert coached basketball with the help of Assistant Coach George Andrews.

Almost from the start in 1968, CBJC placed a priority on athletics, with men's and women's basketball teams. President Huitt Barfoot coached the first year as the teams competed against local colleges.

formed around its outreach to working adults who desired college coursework with a Christian worldview. An early CBJC graduate was Ted Samples, who served a lifetime of pastorates. He was already in his thirties when he gave himself to ministry, and he held other jobs throughout his education and ministries. At times he would ride a 200-mile circuit on Sundays, preaching in various communities. He mostly served Native Americans whose lives were crushed by oppression.[9]

1. L. David Beckman, *Rockmont Horizon* 2.2 (September 1963), 1–2.

2. David L. Beckman, "Letter to Our Immediate Neighbors," October 9, 1967, Clifton Fowler Library archive, CCU.

3. Ron Merryman, e-mail to the author, October 16, 2013.

4. Stanley Toussiant, "From the President's Pen," *Western Witness* (October 1968), 2.

5. Herr had worked as an announcer with the Central Alaska Mission and had been on the student staff at Moody Bible Institute's WMBI.

6. "The Impossible Dream," *Western Witness* (April 1971), 4.

7. Huitt Barfoot, letter to the author, August 28, 2009.

8. Huitt Barfoot, unpublished autobiography, Chapter XIV, n.p., Clifton Fowler Library archive, CCU.

9. Dave Samples, davesamples.blogspot.com, June 1, 2007, accessed July 22, 2010.

CHAPTER 8

Three Streams
1969–1984

Colorado Baptist Junior College

When Huitt Barfoot was engaging support for CBJC, he found a great friend and supporter in Ernie Waite, the pastor of the First Southern Baptist Church in Westminster. The church campus had enough classrooms to house the start-up evening school, and Waite's understanding of the needs of Christian ministers in the area supported a growing student body. Another key founding member was Everett V. Thurman, who served as president until 1983.

CBJC awarded its first diplomas in 1972. In 1977, CBJC moved to the Rose Acres

Colorado Baptist Basketball.

Estate Mansion behind Truett Memorial Church in Edgewater, which had housed the Truett Memorial Church's offices. As the school developed, it took on the name Colorado Baptist College (CBC) and awarded its first college degrees in 1983. Early in 1984, CBC agreed to go without a president for lack of funds. Philip T. Card, a long-time supporter of the school, served as acting president.

Linda Rush joined CBC in 1983 as academic dean and began to pursue North Central accreditation. In the summer of 1984, four interested Southern Baptist laymen offered to contribute a significant sum of money to address the accreditation and financial problems of the school. They required all board members resign while they assessed and reorganized the school. Board members, realizing the precarious position of the school, complied. When this new committee realized accreditation was unattainable because of insufficient financial resources, they sought affiliation with Southwest Baptist University of Bolivar, Missouri.

The autumn of 1984 blew fresh, hopeful changes for CBC: the school settled into its new location at 11111 Mississippi Avenue in Aurora, Colorado; gave its charter to Southwest Baptist University (becoming an extension program of SBU); and re-organized under a board of regents. Colorado Baptist continued its strong Southern Baptist foundation. At this time, CBC had fifty-one students enrolled (twenty full time), and it offered classes late afternoons and weekends. Southwest Baptist supported the school's efforts to develop a new curriculum and an expansion of CBC's mission. Under this fresh arrangement, CBC became Colorado Baptist University.

Western Bible Institute

WBI was granted associate membership in the American Association of Bible Colleges (AABC) beginning March 28, 1969. However, a surprising announcement offset this good news: Dr. Toussaint resigned in the spring of 1969 less than a year into his presidency.

Dr. Paul Wright, a professor, led the college as interim president while he also served as academic dean. As WBI gained a higher profile in Denver through its radio station KWBI, it began an extension school in Colorado Springs in which students could earn a Bible diploma. After more than two years of searching, WBI named Adrian House as the new president beginning in January of 1972. House was a distinguished teacher, pastor, and popular speaker and evangelist whose energy and innovation paid tribute to Carl C. Harwood's vision for WBI.

Under Professor Paul Borden, WBI also started a competitive basketball program. The team played in the Littleton Industrial League, finishing the season with a 10-7 win-loss record. With growing confidence, WBI applied for membership in the Denver Mountain League, which included many regional colleges.

On October 28, 1974, the American Association of Bible Colleges awarded WBI full accreditation. This confirmation of WBI's program would lead to a new name: Western Bible College (WBC), which took effect in July 1975.

In February 1975, WBC signed a cooperative agreement with Fort Hays State College (Kansas), which instituted a program in which a student would attend WBC for two years and then transfer up to sixty-four semester hours of credit

President Adrian House

President Adrian House.

WBI's fourth appointed president was Adrian House, a thirty-six-year-old energetic preacher who recently had been teaching at Biola College and Talbot Theological Seminary in California. The appointment was greeted by cheers from the WBI student body.

He was known for helping small churches in Nebraska and Wyoming and as an evangelist in demand for Bible conferences, evangelistic meetings, and youth conferences across the western states. A former marine, House was trained at Biola College and Denver Theological Seminary.

House was married to Juanita Hummell, whose mother Bonnetta Hummell was a dorm mother for WBI long before he became the new president of WBI.[1]

KWBI

Moving the KWBI transmitter to Mount Chief.

To gain a greater range of broadcasting, KWBI sought to place a radio transmitter on Mount Chief, a location that soared 3,000 feet over Denver, making it the then-highest radio transmitter on the Front Range. Because of the rugged terrain, all materials had to be airlifted by helicopter.[2] Transmission from this transmitter began at 10:00 a.m. on February 15, 1980.

On June 27, 1980, a maintenance truck accidentally snagged a guide wire, which caused the collapse of the old radio tower on WBC's campus. No one was injured, and KWBI incurred only a twelve-minute hiatus in broadcasting.

1972

Graduating

Seniors

David C. Bober
Littleton, Colo.
Diploma
Isa. 40:31

Gerald W. Hartman
Mission Hills, Kan.
B.B.E.
Rev. 3:8

Lois Ann Jennings
Ulysses, Kansas
B.B.E.
Phil. 3:8

Howard L. Langston
Modesto, Calif.
B.A.B.E.
Prov. 3:4, 5

John M. LaRue
Frisco, Colo.
B.B.E.
Phil. 1:6

Charles E. Lawson
Lexington, Neb.
B.B.E.
John 13:34, 35

Mary Lou Lundgren
Kuln, N. Dakota
Diploma
Phil. 1:6

David B. Murphy
Wheatridge, Colo.
B.B.E.
I John 4:4

Charles W. Robinette
Englewood, Colo.
B.A.B.E.
Lam. 3:21-24

Jerry L. Romprey
Coronado, Calif.
B.B.E.
I Cor. 16:14 (NASV)

Jean Marie Salstrom
Dallas, Texas
Diploma
I Sam. 12:24

Lee A. Stubblefield
Logan, Kansas
B.A.B.E.
Phil. 4:19

Judith Rae Woodill
Denver, Colorado
Diploma
II Cor. 3:18

to Fort Hays State. Fort Hays State at the time had over forty major fields. Upon completion of the program (four years total), students would receive two degrees, one from WBC in Bible and one from Fort Hays State in a selected major. This agreement meant that by the fall of 1975, students could choose among several programs: a one-year Bible program for post-high school students, a two-year program in cooperation with Fort Hays State, and a three-year diploma for ministry. In addition, WBC offered a four-year program for a bachelor's degree in Bible, with an emphasis in pastoral studies, missions, Christian education, or sacred music.

Through academics, athletics, and radio outreach, the mid-1970s found WBC surging forward in its work to train students in the Bible. Within five years, the student body and faculty doubled and entered a new phase

Left: WBI graduating seniors, 1972.

Below: Western Bible College and the Denver skyline.

The Western Bible Gang, 1982.

Student fun.

Moving the Prayer Chapel.

Video Programming and Television

In October 1977, WBC conceived a new media branch, the Christian Video Network. Its goal was "to bring a variety of Christian TV programs to the public through cable TV systems throughout the Rocky Mountain area and Midwest." This network operated as a distribution service by receiving and sending to local TV stations tapes of gospel programs and a wide range of wholesome family viewing.[3]

By February 1978, the Christian Video Network had expanded its programming to Casper, Wyoming, providing eight hours of programming each week. In addition, video production facilities at WBC's campus sought to produce original programming.[4]

of financial stability that facilitated campus growth. The school broke ground on married student apartments, and a president's house was purchased and relocated from a nearby dam project.

When President Adrian House completed his leadership, the school had made great strides forward. Bill Boyd, who had been on faculty at WBC for about ten years, was appointed as interim president and then president.

President Boyd had a dream: WBC would offer Christian teacher education beginning in 1979. Boyd had chaired the Christian education program and he saw the need to increase opportunities for women in ministry. The Christian Day School movement was mushrooming, and WBC used the new Christian teacher education program to produce qualified Christian teachers who were grounded in the Scriptures with a biblical philosophy of education.

Practical Christian Work Assignments

Under the direction of Bill Boyd, sophomore students moved across the Denver area to practice sharing their faith. Boyd sought to keep students spiritually alive and hungry and to develop the basic skills of evangelism. The students responded at first with trepidation, but they came to cherish these experiences.

Paul Biggers was assigned to visit patients at the Denver General Hospital:

> Each Sunday afternoon I, along with three other students from Western, go to Denver General Hospital to visit with the patients....Last Sunday, I had the opportunity of leading two men to a saving faith in Christ. Such an experience as this makes our ministry so worthwhile. When a lost soul is brought into God's family, God repays in ways which are indescribable. Certainly our time is not spent in vain.[5]

Charles Robinette was assigned to talk with students on the University of Denver campus:

> My first reaction to hearing that I would have to go to the D. U. campus once a week was that of apprehension.... [Then] I began to see it, not as a job, but as an opportunity to meet people that I wouldn't meet otherwise....Another good aspect of this ministry is that of the learning involved. I often find that I don't know as much as I thought I did. Just because I passed a Doctrine exam with an A or B doesn't mean that I know it well enough to communicate it. I usually find myself going back home to find answers to questions or restudying something from one of my classes.[6]

President Bill Boyd.

Recognition of the education program followed. In August 1979 the Association of Christian Schools International (ACSI) accredited WBC under provisional status, and WBC retained its accreditation with the American Association of Bible Colleges.

In their senior year, 1980–1981, thirty-eight graduates of WBC celebrated the addition of women's volleyball to the athletic program. However, the most exciting announcement was a new youth ministries major, a rare program among Christian colleges. Building on its focus on Christian education, WBC also sought to launch a system of Christian schools in kindergarten through sixth grade in the Denver area and provide direction, supervision, procurement of teachers, and curriculum planning for participating churches.

WBC Student Union.

WBC Snack Bar.

The 1981–1982 academic year pushed programs to a new level. In the winter of 1982, WBC launched a graduate program in theology-Bible and an external video studies (EVS) program. The target students for the graduate program included people who sought a year of intensive Bible courses before serving in ministry.

Student Fun at WBC

In the winter of 1979, students used the light of the full moon to shovel piles of snow in front of classroom doors, effectively cancelling classes for a day. Paul Flannery confesses the "crime" in his poem, "The Tale of the 'Pit' and the Full Moon." Several stanzas read,

We crouched, we snuck with shovel in hand.

A thrill and excitement united this band.

By stealth we crept closer and closer to the place

Where teachers and rulers controlled and plotted our fates.

Homework and more, they worked us into the night.

This time just once we'd show them who's right.

We shoveled and threw the new fallen snow.

Higher and higher the piles did grow.

The EVS program served two groups: service personnel, who desired to study the Bible for college credit via videotape at Overseas Christian Servicemen's Centers, and teachers in schools certified by the Association of Christian Schools International. WBC's influence reached around the globe.

After several years of innovative success President Boyd resigned in 1983. Frank

WBC students.

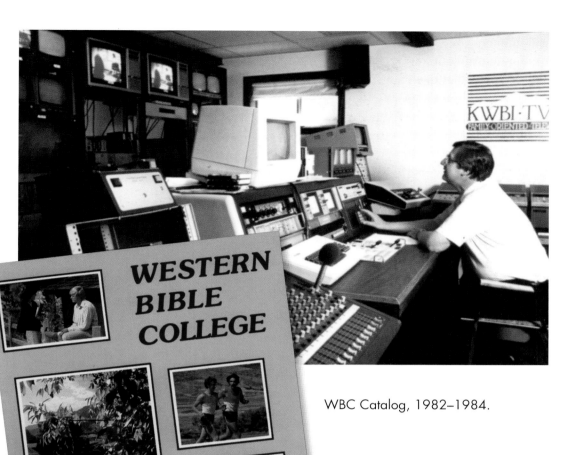

Television ministry.

WBC Catalog, 1982–1984.

Ames, academic vice president; Roland Heib, from the broadcasting network; and Rick Pinkham, business manager, served on an interim committee to administrate WBC pending the selection of a new president.

WBC staff, 1984.

Rockmont campus.

Rockmont

After its 1967 move to Lakewood and unable to sell its Longmont campus, Rockmont entered the 1970s under severe financial distress. After selling a portion of its forty-three acres to a commercial medical project (which never developed[7]) and securing its Longmont property to the Reynolds family who held an unpaid balance on the Lakewood property, Rockmont limped through the first few years of the 1970s.

Although hundreds of private colleges in America closed their doors during this decade, Rockmont survived for four reasons, according to President Beckman: Rockmont's small size limited operating costs; dedicated staff and faculty stayed despite delayed paychecks; para-church ministries led by Dr. Beckman provided

income; and God clearly guided and provided. One such blessing was the donation by movie star Ernest Borgnine of a thirty-seven-foot cabin cruiser, which sold for $12,000 in 1970.[8]

For a second time in less than a decade, the Rockmont and WBI boards discussed a merger in 1971. Although Dr. Beckman supported a merger, he recommended they should defer action until program and facilities issues could be discussed. The April and May 1971 faculty minutes from Rockmont record some of the obstacles; faculty acknowledged that although Rockmont would benefit financially from a merger with WBI, the restrictions of the merger were dissuasive. WBI would require fifty to fifty-five semester hours of Bible and would allow a liberal arts program only as "areas of concentration," not as majors. The proposed plan was a considerable concession for both schools. WBI's program of study at the time required 103.5 quarter-hours of Bible and theological subjects and thirty-eight quarter-hours in the arts. Rockmont, on the other hand, required forty-eight quarter-hours in Bible and fifty-six in the arts, other than courses in a major.

The faculty at Rockmont resisted turning the liberal arts college back into a Bible school. However, Rockmont's board tried to persuade the faculty to accept the benefits of a merger. Dean Harold Miller wrote to Board Chairman Harold Williamson, "Please believe me. I am not arguing against the merger. I am terribly disturbed about the proposed *conditions* of the merger."

Gene Marlatt, assistant professor of social science at Rockmont, reiterated some of Miller's concerns, but he added that the move to WBI's campus would be "suicidal" to the college's appeal to metropolitan commuter students. In addition, WBI viewed Rockmont's student policies as lax because they admitted students whose beards and jeans disturbed the conservative

Dr. Gene Marlatt.

expectations of a Christian college. In the end, the board and the faculty of Rockmont decided such a proposed merger with WBI would not be a merger at all, but an absorption into WBI.

What benefit came of these discussions? In their effort to overcome the financial difficulties without the possibility of the merger, Rockmont administrators offered creative solutions. Toward the end of one faculty and board discussion at Rockmont, a seed was planted to begin a new kind of school within the college, which came to fruition in 1973 under Marlatt's direction.

Marlatt's work was forward thinking for the era, and the school came to be called the School of Innovative Studies, retaining this moniker until the late 1990s. This move into adult education would help Rockmont survive future financial tests, but it also opened up educational opportunities for non-traditional students who sought convenient locations and course offerings, credentialing for professional purposes, and a full college experience that fit into their already busy adult lives. In the first year, twenty students enrolled, and the numbers increased to over one hundred the following year.

Another encouraging means of God's providence arrived in a bequest from a brother/sister couple who had no heirs and left their estate of $350,000 to Rockmont. This couple had treasured a relationship they had formed with a Rockmont student in the 1950s. Rockmont paid back salaries with interest, settled outstanding bills, and used the leftover funds to create a library wing and chapel in 1974.

Although financial pressure and property concerns stressed the administration of Rockmont, the college's focus remained on

Rockmont College

Within the shadows of the majestic Colorado Rocky Mountains lies the picturesque campus of Rockmont, a Christian liberal arts college of distinction. Since 1914, Rockmont has given itself wholeheartedly to men and women seeking creative educational experiences of excellence, preparing students of diverse denominational and ethnic backgrounds to confront the future with firm commitments to Biblical Christianity.

Rockmont's 33 acre campus is situated on the southwestern edge of Denver. It includes two lakes, nestled within a gently rolling terrain, scores of cottonwood, willow and pine, and acres of open space ideal for soccer, softball, volleyball and archery. The entire expanse lends symmetry to Rockmont's Spanish-style learning center, which houses the chapel, performance center, classroom complex, library, student lounge, dining hall and administration offices. Within this context, a partnership of immeasureable impact can take place: Rockmont and You.

Viewbook is a preview of such a partnership. We think you'll see the differences which make Rockmont a school of unique opportunities. We believe our distinctiveness is sound reasoning for considering Rockmont as the college of your choice.

Rockmont brochure.

enabling students to change the world. For instance, the counterculture movement of the 1960s and '70s was met by the Jesus Movement and what '70s vernacular called "street Christians"—believers who came out of the hippie and drug culture. Rockmont opened its admission to street Christians even though this move disrupted the "appearance" of Rockmont students to the public.

In another example, the Beckman family housed two young men who did not fit into the crowded dorm. One of them later shared that rooming in "Dr. B's" study meant that "one had to deal with the feeling upon waking of having taken up lodging in a library by mistake….What a wonderful example to us of the grace of our Lord that we found there!" Aunt Hett (Dr. Beckman's

aunt) claimed these two young men as boyfriends, a special "consolation to our then-dateless souls."

By 1974, Rockmont was back on solid footing, strong enough to gain candidate status for regional accreditation in the North Central Association of Colleges and Schools. Looking forward, Rockmont began plans to expand with new classrooms and an administrative center, a maintenance building, and student housing—three apartment buildings that would later be named after Archie Yetter, Carl C. Harwood Sr., and Ernie Waite, pioneers in CCU's three heritage schools.[9]

Along with expanding the physical plant, Rockmont geared up for new majors. In 1975, Rockmont offered majors in history,

Rockmont student apartments.

DISCOVER YOURSELF SKIING

BIBLE
LIBERAL
ARTS
BASKETBALL
DRAMA
MUSIC
NCAA SKI
TEAM

Rockmont College
8801 W. Alameda Ave. - Denver, CO 80226 - 303-238-5386

Rockmont skiing.

A Competitive Ski Team at Rockmont

The 1974–1975 school year saw the addition of a ski team to the two intercollegiate sports already offered: basketball and soccer. Rockmont competed against eight Colorado colleges and universities, as well as the University of New Mexico. Under the coaching of Neil Wokodoff, the team practiced at Geneva Basin, and one of the skiers, Art Kinch, later skied for Costa Rica in Olympic competitions.

Bible, psychology, missions, music, and Christian education. The long-range plan called for the development of new majors by 1982: biology, sociology, drama, humanities, music, business, and state-recognized teacher certification. Sports remained a staple of school recognition with a new ski team, and Rockmont began a new student newspaper, the *Rockmont Observer*.

By 1981, Rockmont achieved full accreditation from the North Central

Association, and it followed this confirmation of its quality programs by adding a new outreach in 1982: non-traditional education. Teachers seeking recertification credit enrolled in these accelerated weekend courses, with more than one hundred new students attending the inaugural courses.

Completing nearly twenty years of strong leadership through lean times and bountiful provision by God, President Beckman retired from Rockmont and was awarded president emeritus status. Rockmont's board named Dr. William

Wilkie as the new Rockmont president. Wilkie had an early career as a faculty member at Michigan State University before he served as a special assistant to the president of MSU. In addition, he had experience working with the W.K. Kellogg Foundation and as an executive in the automotive supplier industry. When he was called to be president of Rockmont College beginning in October 1982, the board of directors of Rockmont charged him with three goals: to eliminate short-term debt, to introduce sound educational and business practices, and to create a new mission for Rockmont.

---

1. "Adrian House—WBI's Fourth President," *Western Witness* (October 1971), 3.

2. "KWBI Transmitter Re-Location," *Western Witness* (November 1979), 1.

3. "New Video Branch of WBC Brings Gospel to Television," *Western Witness* (October 1977), 3.

4. "CVN on the Air in Casper," *Western Witness* (February 1978), 1.

5. "Giving Away Their Faith," *Western Witness* (February 1969), 4–5.

6. Ibid.

7. According to Lew Price '55 (a Rockmont board member), Harold Williamson and seventeen others

formed the Garrison Group, who purchased land from Humana and private parties for $12,500 per acre and sold it later to Mile Hi Church for $100,000 per acre. Proceeds went to Rockmont. A warranty deed executed May 24, 1983, records a vacant land sale to Mile Hi for $446,925.

8. Ernest Borgnine won an Oscar in 1955 and was the beloved Lieutenant Commander Quinton McHale in *McHale's Navy* (TV series, 1960s). A relative of Dr. Beckman's wife Bev referred him to Rockmont when he wanted to donate his yacht to a charity.

9. The original names for these residence halls were Alpha, Beta, and Gamma.

CCU AND HERITAGE SCHOOL BOARD MEMBERS

Over the last century, God has blessed Colorado Christian University with admirable men and women who have been called to serve as trustees of CCU and its heritage institutions. With the passage of time, our records are not complete, but these are some of those chosen by God to lead the university over the last one hundred years.

C. "Andy" Anderson

Ellen M. Armstrong

Gary E. Armstrong

William L. Armstrong

Toby P. Cole

Terry Considine

Charles Cutforth

James S. Dixon

Larry Donnithorne

Margaret A. Fomer

Kaye Lynn Fote

Don M. Harwell

Stanley A. Harwood

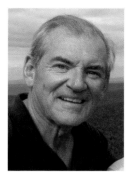

K. Mike Henshaw

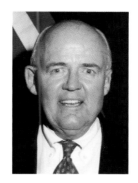

R. Ed Johnson

Dr. William Cody	James S. Dixon	Kaye Lynn Fote
Bernald Coffin	Dick Dodge	Clifton L. Fowler
Toby P. Cole	David Donaldson	L. J. Fowler
Vaughn Cole	Larry Donnithorne	Stan Fredericks
Charles Collins	Robert P. Dugan Jr.	Keith Fredrickson
Paul Conant	Tom Dunkerton	William J. Girvin
Terry Considine	Ralph N. Eberhardt	Pauline Glover
John Couch	Art Edmunds	Richard T. Godwin
Lloyd Crawford	Arlo Edmundson	W. Ray Gorsage
Charles Cutforth	Carla Elam-Floyd	Dougal Graham
George W. Cutrell	George Esch	E. H. Graves
Gordon Dahl	J. H. Estep	Joshua Gravett
Maurice Dametz	B. E. Etherton	Leroy Green
Floyd J. Davis	Frank W. Farmer	Jim Groen
H. A. Davis	Ruel Farwell	Merl Grogan
Hale V. Davis	Delbert Fehsenfeld	James R. Gunlock
John D. Deakins	Elsie Fick	Frank Haas
Eldon Decker	Helen Fick	F. Donald Hall
R. L. Decker	William A. Fick	Ronald Hanson
A. R. DePriest	George B. Fletcher	E. Harold Harper
Bob DeWolf	Margaret A. Fomer	Ronald Harris
John W. Dick	Dr. James Forrester	Walter H. Harris
E. B. Dickey	Gerald Foster	Don M. Harwell

Tim Kenczewicz

Sam Kimbriel

Harold A. "Hal" Krause

Chick Lee

Terry Leprino

Stanley K. Mann

Christine C. Mastin

Gerald W. May

Gordon Mayberry

Douglas I. McDonald

Donald MacDonald
Stanley K. Mann
Charles B. Marsh
William R. Marshall
John Marwin
Christine C. Mastin
Jim Mather
Gerald W. May
Gordon Mayberry
Lyle Mayhew
John L. McCartney
William Avery McClure
Robert McCollum
W. G. McConnell
Douglas McDonald
Lee McDowell
Gary McIntosh
S. T. McKinney
Glenn McMahan
Bob McPhearson
Tim McTavish
Ronald C. Merryman

Marilyn Metz
W. James Metz
Herman F. Meyers
Roy Miller
Carroll D. Mitchell
Fenton Moorhead
Alvin Morgan
J. E. Morrison
Roderick Morrison
B. Franklin Moss Jr.
Charles Mueller
Susan Mueller
Virginia Mullin
Harley Mullins
Roy G. Munroe
Dave Myers
Carl W. Nelson
Harvey R. Nelson
Russell F. Nelson
Harold New
William G. Newer
L. Norris

Vigil Nyberg
William G. Nyman
Kenneth W. Ogden
George W. Olinger
Ivan E. Olsen
Carl G. Olson
Vernon Olson
Robert Oxford
Marco Padilia
Wayne Parsons
William Pauls
Arvel Payne
Henry G. Pelon
Ernest L. Perrine
Elmer H. Peterson
Kenneth Peterson
Claud M. Pettit
Phillip Philibosian
S. L. Power
James P. Presba
Lew Price
Walt Rakowich

Lee McDowell

Tim McTavish

Susan Mueller

Kenneth W. Ogden

William Pauls

Claud M. Pettit

Lew Price

Walt Rakowich

Verley G. Sangster

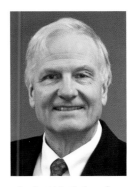
Dale W. Schaefer

Thomas N. Scheffel

Donald Siecke

Gerald R. Stafford

Donald W. Sweeting

Kenell J. Touryan

John A. Turner

William J. White

Robert L. Woodson Sr.

Elmer Seger
Mr. Sewell
Clyde Shaffstall
William Shea
Donald Siecke
John Sigvaldson
L. L. Silkensen
Richard J. Singewald
W. Randall Skillen Jr.
Jim Smallwood
Merwyn Smith
Thomas C. Sorensen
Jack Sparks
H. A. Sprague
Gerald R. Stafford
Robert Starr
Carle Stenmark
W. Stephens
Donald W. Sweeting
Willard Taussig
Everett Thruman

O. C. Ramey
Ray Ransom
J. O. Record
John C. Reeves
Charles Renstrom
Ruby Renstrom
William P. Renstrom
John "Jack" Robinson
H. C. Rodgers
Byron G. Rogers
Ralph W. Rowe

Stanley Sandberg
Irvin W. Sanders
Randy Sanders
Verley G. Sangster
Leroy Sargant
Dale W. Schaefer
Allen Paul Schantz
Thomas N. Scheffel
G. J. Schilperoort
Ronald Schmidt
Ed Seaberg

1914 — Clifton Fowler founds Denver Bible Institute (DBI, later DBC).

1948 — Carl C. Harwood founds Western Bible Institute (WBI, later WBC).

1949 — Denver Bible College becomes Rockmont College and moves to Longmont in 1954, then to Lakewood in 1967.

1960 — WBI moves its campus to Jefferson County, near Morrison.

1968 — Huitt Barfoot founds Colorado Baptist Junior College (CBJC, later CBC).

1984 — Rockmont and WBC merge, creating Colorado Christian College (CCC).

1985 — Colorado Baptist College becomes Colorado Baptist University (CBU), an extension program of Southwest Baptist University.

1957 Rockmont Board

Kenell J. Touryan

William A. Trimble

J. Nelson Truitt

Paul G. Tschetter

John A. Turner

Fay C. Van

Wendell E. Vance

Luis Villarreal

Carl Vogel

P. J. Von Westenberg

Ernest Waite

Joe Wall

Arlene Warren

Don Warren

Dennis K. Wells

Robert Wells

Don Whipple

William J. White

George R. Whiting

William P. Whittemore

William Wilkie

Donald K. Wilkin

Keith Williams

Harold Williamson

Harold A. Wilson

W. Michael Wilson

Joe D. Wise Jr.

Donald Wolf

Charles B. Wood

Robert L. Woodson Sr.

S. Parker Woolmington

Archie H. Yetter

Angelo L. "Bud" Zanett

Michael Zastrocky

President Skillen and Board

1989

CCC and CBU merge, creating Colorado Christian University (CCU).

1990

The University's athletic teams compete in the Rocky Mountain Athletic Conference (RMAC), Division II.

2002

The College of Adult and Graduate Studies (CAGS) restructures and will include campuses in Colorado Springs, Denver Tech Center, Grand Junction, Lakewood, Loveland, Northglenn, and online education.

2010

CCU's Centennial Institute launches the first Western Conservative Summit.

2014

CCU celebrates 100 years of innovative Christian higher education.

CHAPTER 9

Joining Hands:
College Mergers in the 1980s

Stan Harwood, former president of the board of WBI, recalled that the original idea for a merger with Rockmont began in 1965 when he had talked with Bill Bernsten, president of Northwestern College in Minnesota. "You're too small," Bernsten said. "You need to get bigger and have more of an impact upon the community." He suggested WBI merge with Rockmont, the only other Christian evangelical college in the region.[1] Dr. Beckman, the president of Rockmont at that time, met with Harwood. However, the faculty of Rockmont voted not to merge and the WBI administration believed the individual philosophies of the schools could not mesh.

In 1971, leaders of WBI and Rockmont again considered a merger, when Paul Wright led WBI. By this time, Rockmont had established its campus in Lakewood. The discussion progressed, but the differences between the two institutions had broadened. However, as both schools developed their own programs and outreaches, they became much closer in their educational philosophy.

In 1984, President Wilkie sought a way to pay off Rockmont's debts by dissolving the resident campus. Wilkie had planned to use part of the proceeds to establish a foundation that would help put Christian students through other schools in Colorado.[2] On February 15, 1984, Rockmont's board voted to close the school. Immediately, faculty and alumni led a heroic effort to save Rockmont and raise needed funds. Wilkie

President Wilkie. *From* Reflections 82–83, *the Rockmont yearbook.*

President Joe Wall.

Rockmont College
180 South Garrison, Denver, Colorado 80226
(303) 238-5386

Rockmont auction ticket, 1985.

resigned from the presidency and after the brief interim presidency of Professor Gene Marlatt, Dr. Beckman was invited to lead Rockmont again.

While Rockmont was in the throes of financial ruin and reorganization, WBC faced leadership challenges. President Boyd resigned from WBC in 1983, and a presidential search resulted in an invitation to Dr. Joe Wall, who declined. But Wall said God would not let him rest in this decision—literally. For the next three nights Wall woke from a dream in which he was telling a crowd of people he could not be their president, much to their disappointment. The dream convicted him, and after a week of prayer he realized God was leading him to Colorado.[3]

With Dr. Wall as president of WBC, a merger with a liberal arts college appeared more possible. Instead of creating obstacles, the problems both colleges faced made them more compatible. Presidents Beckman and Wall became friends and colleagues, and the weakened financial state of Rockmont did not daunt the president of WBC. Neither did WBC's earlier staunch position against the liberal arts discourage Beckman. "I think a merger could have great potential," Beckman said in an article for the school paper. "Both schools have a lot to offer each other. Each has programs that would be enhanced by a merger – it is almost as if our strengths and weaknesses fit perfectly together."

The idea of a merger was ready for negotiation. Beckman and Marlatt were the primary negotiators for Rockmont while Wall and Frank Ames, vice president for academic affairs, represented WBC. The doctrinal statements for each school were different, but this issue was worked out, causing some turmoil in the respective faculties.

The leaders of the merger invited the members of each school's faculty to teach at the new college, as long as faculty members could agree with the statement of faith and philosophy of education. Various faculty members on both sides were resistant to the requirement of signing the new doctrinal statement; for some the statement seemed ultraconservative and for others it seemed too broad. Only a few professors, including Cap Hensley, a popular religion professor, did not sign the statement and did not receive a teaching contract for the merged school.

Dr. Beckman was appointed as chancellor to work closely with Dr. Wall, who would be president. Marlatt from Rockmont was appointed the new academic advisor and Ames from WBC the academic dean. In order to ensure fairness, the merged board consisted of the same number of members from each school.

Merging programs caused some concern because both schools wanted to retain their accreditations: North Central Association and the American Association of Bible Colleges. In order to keep WBC's accreditation with AABC, the merged institution would require thirty hours of Bible for all majors. In order to keep NCA accreditation achieved by Rockmont, Beckman would remain president of the merged institution for the first few months and "Bible" would not be included in the new name. Rockmont kept its liberal arts curriculum and WBC kept its strong biblical studies and Christian ministries programs.[4]

Neither campus was sold in the end, but all parties debated which home the future college would have. Faculty from both schools submitted arguments for their own locations. Finally, Beckman suggested the combined campus be started in Lakewood, with its superior facilities, and over a period of time the WBC campus in the foothills could be improved and occupied. Until then, WBC's campus could be used for conferences and special events.

Students were unsure about the merger. Ray Brown, a sophomore drama major, told the *Rocky Mountain News* he was worried about the style of the new school and the implications of the merger. He chose to attend Rockmont because he felt it was an "open place" in which to be educated. Graduating students from WBC, on the other hand, requested President Wall make the graduation address at the first commencement ceremonies because they desired to end the year with the president they had known.

Wall addressed the concerns of students from both former institutions in his own interview for the school paper when he said, "The environment at the school is one in which all students are Christians. We must learn how to be understanding and tolerant of the differences in beliefs others may have."[5]

In the end, the new institution was called "Colorado Christian College" (CCC). After a brief summer with Beckman as president, Wall was president of the new school for the next six years.

CCC emblem.

Colorado Christian College, 1988.

The merger provided a diverse student body with great energy and opportunities for ministry. Residential students lived in the stairwells, and they created their own fun with such events as the Lip Sync Contest. The music groups were Crossfire, a "high energy Christian rock band;" Mainstream, CCC's techno-pop rock group; and the Colorado Christian College Choir, who toured the West Coast in May of 1986.

Colorado Christian College

CCC postcard. *Courtesy of Joe L. Brown and now part of the CCU archive.*

CCC Ski Club.

Alpha Psi Omega, an honorary fraternity for drama, continued from its Rockmont days. The drama team put on *Royal Gambit* and one-act plays. A new dance troupe was formed, the Karar Dance Company. The new newspaper was called the *CCC Chronicle*. For athletics, CCC offered a flag football team, men's basketball, women's basketball, and a ski club. For non-competitive athletics, the Outdoor Fanatics Club was born.

CCC expressed its spiritual unity through regular chapels. Students who formerly led the Missions Impact Club from WBC formed the Student Missionary Fellowship of CCC, which met weekly for prayer. However, students agreed the most unifying day was Festival '85, a fall event filled with music, games, and spiritual fun. The artists and audience "kept the CCC

CCC students, 1986.

CCC student fun.

campus rockin', rollin', boogeyin' and shakin' till four minutes past ten o-clock," records the yearbook staff of the 1985 *Cross Current*. "Only the expiration of the city noise permit was responsible for the seemingly early benediction, appropriately closing in prayer a day in the Son and an evening of unity."

A Second Merger

While Rockmont and WBC negotiated the merger, Colorado Baptist College was about to begin its new life as an extension program of Southwest Baptist University in Bolivar, Missouri. In 1985, the college was renamed Colorado Baptist University. With strong support and guidance from its supporting institution, CBU grew quickly and sought to move into a residential campus, the former Colorado Women's College in Denver. Work groups from around the U.S. poured onto the campus to paint, repair, and prepare the campus for fall enrollment, and the official move in was scheduled for June 1, 1987.

Optimism ran so high that CBU considered buying the old Loretto Heights College campus in Denver. The euphoria and rapid growth that followed what seemed to be a permanent, positive move was quietly dashed as Southwest Baptist withdrew its support of CBU by 1989. Some educational philosophies at Southwest Baptist had changed with a new administration, and the extension program in Colorado was no longer sustainable. CBU realized it needed to gain North Central accreditation on its own, which was unlikely. By January 1989, CBU was in the process of phasing out its daytime programs and planned to return to teaching evening adult classes. In addition, CBU began discussions with CCC about a merger.

This negotiation process with CCC moved quickly. The final yearbook for CBU is titled *Wings of Promise,* and it suggests that the merger was finalized: "Why is our future so bright we've gotta wear shades? Well, not only will we begin

CBU campus.

a new semester next year, but we will also attend a new university: Colorado Christian University. Naturally, there will be several compromises that will take place; the joining of two similar but very different schools requires compromise. The purposes for the merge vary and so do the responses from both the administration and the students, but through it all, we anticipate one great get-together."

And a great get-together it was. CCC in effect absorbed CBU, gaining CBUs debts, its faculty and students, and the energy from the Eagles and Lady Eagles sports teams. CBU had an

CCC Basketball.

CBU Women's Volleyball.

athletic director, competed in the National Association of Intercollegiate Athletics conference, and brought to CCC men's and women's basketball programs, men's and women's soccer programs, and a women's volleyball team that had been coached by CBU's chaplain, Dr. Woody Northcutt.

The newly merged institution was named Colorado Christian University in 1989.

Master of Arts in Biblical Counseling Program

CCU acquired an immediate national reputation in 1989 through its affiliation with Dr. Larry Crabb's Christian counseling program that formerly had been housed at

Grace Theological Seminary in Winona Lake, Indiana. Crabb had served on the faculty of Grace, chairing a similar program there for seven years. When Grace's mission became inhospitable to "Christian psychology," he sought a new home for the program and contacted President Wall, whom he had met at a conference. Wall and the board approved. Crabb brought with him from Grace Seminary Dr. Dan Allender and Dr. Tom Varney and served as the chair of the master of arts in biblical counseling program (MABC) at CCU for eight years.

The MABC program was housed on the old campus where WBC had held classes and where the radio station KWBI operated its metro Denver station. The Crabbs spruced up the campus and invested their

Dr. Larry Crabb.

own money in buying a phone system and a copier for the new work.

The program grew faster than Crabb had envisioned, with fifty to ninety students enrolled from the United States and around the world. Within a decade, educational philosophies among the MABC faculty began to diverge, with Allender taking on a professional model for counseling and Crabb taking on a shepherding model. Crabb resigned as chair, but remained on as a professor. Beginning in the late 1990s, he

The WBI campus houses the new MABC program.

serves as distinguished scholar in residence at CCU, participating in special seminars and radio spots for the university.[6]

In September of 1989, CCU had a traditional undergraduate program of 559 students, continuing education programs in Lakewood and Colorado Springs, and the masters of arts in biblical counseling on the Morrison campus.

1. Stan Harwood, interview with Ken Gire, October 8, 2007.

2. Terry Mattingly, "Religious Colleges Near Merger Pact," *Rocky Mountain News* (November 15, 1985), 8.

3. Joe Wall, interview with Ken Gire, February 18, 2008.

4. Gene Marlatt, Letter to Ken Touryan (Trustee), "Thoughts on the Paradigm for a Fully Merged Western Bible College and Rockmont College: Faculty, Staff, Academic Departments, Majors" (July 20, 1984), Clifton Fowler Library archive, CCU.

5. Joe Wall, "Wall Optimistic; Encourages Involvement," interview by Brad Hicks published in the CCC school newspaper (unnamed), September 6, 1985.

6. Larry Crabb, interview with Ken Gire, February 19, 2008.

CHAPTER 10

University Vision in the 1990s

The Lakewood campus at 180 South Garrison Street remained the best choice for the traditional undergraduate program and the Lakewood hub of the non-traditional adult programs, although professors taught classes across many sites in Colorado. CCU joined the newly formed Colorado Athletic Conference (CAC), consisting of regional colleges and universities: Metro State University, Regis University, the University of Denver, the University of Colorado, Colorado Springs, and the University of Southern Colorado. Just in time for the fall 1990 CAC season, CCU's new gymnasium/field house was completed.

CCU builds a gymnasium.

President Joe Wall with Elsie Fick and Helen Fick.

Basketball fans in 1993.

Dr. David Beckman.

Dr. Richard Beal.

Management in Human Resources

CCU developed the management in human resources program (MHR) in 1990–1991 as outreach to working adults. MHR allowed students who already had a few years of college credit to enroll in the one-year program. Students attended classes one night each week for four hours, with courses arranged in five-week segments. Within a year, all courses necessary for a bachelor's degree were complete. This program allowed working adults to continue their education without sacrificing their jobs, in turn giving them greater opportunities in their careers.

Athletics at CCU featured team sports, including soccer, tennis, basketball, and later cross-country. CCU also allowed individuals to compete. For instance, in 1990–1991, Brian Brock competed for CCU as a cycler

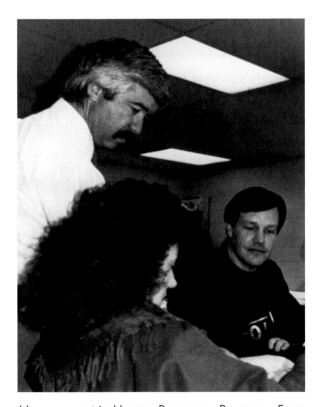

Management in Human Resources Program. *From Diadem 1991, the CCU yearbook.*

and Robert Gelinas represented CCU at track meets.

Cheerleading (1990) and men's golf and cross-country (1995) helped build an overall athletic program. When the University of Denver withdrew from the CAC, leaving it one team shy of being a full conference, the new Rocky Mountain Athletic Conference adopted Colorado teams in 1996, making RMAC the largest Division II conference in the United States.

When President Wall resigned in 1991, Dr. Beckman was invited back to lead the school once again. Under Beckman's leadership, attention was refocused on building academic programs. As student activities demanded growth and flexibility, the faculty was busy working on new

President Ron Schmidt.

The inauguration of President Schmidt.

The 1993 choir concert.

programs for academic expansion. The master of arts in curriculum and instruction program (MACI), intended for teachers needing to gain continuing education credits, was offered starting in 1993.

By 1993, the Colorado State Board of Education approved CCU's programs in secondary education, including middle school and music programs, and an accelerated elementary education program. In 1994, the North Central Association (NCA) approved a new master of science in management degree and in 1996 a master of arts in professional counseling degree.

After the mergers, board member Chuck Lambotte provided a major gift to the university, part of which resulted in a room in what is now called the Beckman Center being reconfigured into a theater. Beckman stepped down from his third tenure as

president of CCU, making way for Ron Schmidt on July 1, 1993.

The university had already begun a significant facilities upgrade. Until the mid-1990s, piles of students' muddy boots could be seen outside classrooms. Some paved sidewalks replaced crisscrossed pathways. The library found a home in the building that had formerly housed the chapel. Schmidt built on this momentum and created an Academic Commons consisting of permanent and temporary buildings on the north side of campus. President Schmidt also assisted in purchasing a church on Garrison Street that became the Music Center. During his tenure, K Marie Stolba began her annual lectures as visiting distinguished professor of music. In 2005–2006, she gave half her estate to CCU.

Woody Northcutt Prayer Chapel.

President Schmidt sought to beautify the campus, making it attractive to prospective students. The campus began again to strain at the seams, with 750 traditional undergrads filling classroom space and vying for the three hundred beds available. Student athletes were housed in a nearby motel.

Schmidt's most important contribution, however, was a vision for a newly built campus on the Morrison property, the fifty-two acres that had been WBI's campus before the merger. Schmidt worked with the board of trustees to gain

The Aspen building is placed.

Students swing into the pond.

an option on ninety-three additional acres adjacent to the property and to seek even more land for relocation. He worked with consultants to envision a campus wholly "Colorado" in atmosphere, with mule deer roaming near village-style offices and classrooms. In order to focus on the new campus plans, President Schmidt created the office of provost, appointing Doug Jackson, who had been the vice president of development.

On January 7, 1997, President Schmidt addressed students and faculty in chapel in which he announced some big changes were in store for CCU. He said, "We cannot afford to put up a

wall around ourselves as a school...." To solve the problems of the "CCU bubble," financial stress, and facility needs, Schmidt advocated admitting non-Christians to the traditional undergraduate program.[1]

Trash Club.

Students play in the pond.

Rolling it on the pond.

Broadcast Communications Outreach from CCU

In the early 1990s, CCU's media outreach gained a new edge with TV-41 added to its list of offerings. Radio stations KJOL FM provided programming for the western slope of the Rocky Mountains from Grand Junction, and KWBI served the Denver metro area. In addition, a co-owned FM translator with KDRH in Glenwood Springs was added to the opportunities.

By 1998, CCU's radio network extended to nearly thirty cities across the Front Range of Colorado, southern Wyoming, western Colorado, some mountain communities, and eastern Utah.

KWBI.

Student response to this proposed change was strong. But perhaps more important than their unhappiness about the modified admission policy, students were frustrated with rapidly rising tuition (about a 20 percent increase), which they suspected would be paying for the new campus development. In fact, the tuition costs seemed to dominate student unrest. The struggle was so severe that an April 1997 *Cougar Trax* article notes a majority of students would not return to campus housing in the fall semester, primarily to save money.

Licensing Program for Educators (LPE) Weekend Course (School of Professional Studies).

Faculty and staff struggled because of the gap between the vision for great advances and the lack of resources. The battle to control few resources caused division among departments and co-curricular areas, and the residual effects were felt into the next decade. Jim McCormick, who came to CCU in 1995, noted that scant resources formed only part of the problem. At the heart, the merged institution had not formed a new, distinct identity and was haunted by unresolved crises from heritage institutions, crippling its advance.[2]

Although unrest on campus was high, several lasting "institutions" started in the spring of 1997. Matt Coleman started the popular "Trash Club," which sought to serve students' needs by regularly collecting trash from student residence halls, while mentoring young men as servant-leaders. "King Cougar" also enjoyed its inaugural performance—a pageant that humorously displayed the talents of male students. Frisbee golf on a campus-wide course provided round-the-clock competition among students.

President Ronald Schmidt resigned from the presidency in June 1997. Dr. Leroy Green, who had been a board member since 1987 and was the chair of the board, was appointed interim president. Green had been a missionary in Zaire, a principal, and a teacher. His tenure as interim president of CCU was short, as the search for the new president resulted in an invitation to Dr. Larry Donnithorne.

When Donnithorne joined the university as president in 1998, CCU offered a wide

Zoning Issues at the Morrison Campus

The Harwood family originally donated a fifty-plus-acre tract of land just west of C470 and south of US 285 to WBI in 1959. Strategic partners of CCU, including members of the board of trustees, orchestrated a series of donations and purchases in the 1990s, expanding the site to 284.4 acres. President Donnithorne said during his tenure there were seven acquisitions of land.[4] In the mid-1990s, President Schmidt worked with a team of architects to envision a Colorado-themed campus on this site.

In 1999 under President Donnithorne's leadership, teams of CCU constituents met with architects to discuss the development of the Morrison property, culminating in a September 1999 competition among architects. However, a rezoning application faced local barriers.

The Hogback Conservancy Coalition, made up of eleven homeowner associations and other local groups, voiced strong, organized opposition. Among their top concerns were the traffic expected on a college campus and the loss of open space.

The Jefferson County Planning Commission voted six to one against CCU's rezoning proposal in the spring of 2002. Concurrently, the administration moved forward with seeking other sites for a new campus and working on a resubmission of a rezoning application.

CCU submitted a new campus plan to the Jefferson County Planning Commission in August 2004, which located the new campus in the eastern valley of the property. The planning commission recommended denial, and CCU withdrew its application.

range of bachelor degree programs in the arts, sciences, and music. Three master degree programs prepared students for professional lives: the master of arts in counseling (biblical or professional tracks), master of science in management, and a master of arts in curriculum and instruction. In addition, CCU had extension programs in the School of Professional Studies in the metro Denver area and across the state.[3] It offered the prestigious Staley Lectures by distinguished scholars who addressed issues of theology, ethics, ministry, and spiritual life.

Even before Donnithorne arrived, the administration of CCU had met with the Jefferson

Technology in the twentieth century.

County Planning Council to develop its formal application to re-zone the additional acres of the Morrison property for new campus development. One of Donnithorne's first presidential memos to the board noted ongoing zoning concerns, which would trouble his administration throughout his tenure.

Technology was a driving factor of some of CCU's development in the late 1990s. The long-promised e-mail service was finally available to students in 1996. Then, 1998 brought two new technological developments. First, CCU would begin offering distance learning programs, beginning with the MBA, which would combine in-seat and online education. Second, the school announced a generous donation from JD Edwards in software to facilitate accounting, human resources, facilities, and online support.

Near the end of the century, the School of Innovative Studies (SIS) transitioned to the School of Professional Studies (SPS). The graduate programs were managed in an uncomfortable area between SPS and the departments in which the courses were offered.

Donnithorne's "Pray and Plan" 1999 campaign was designed to seek out what was the essence of the university. Over the next few years, he led CCU to begin to answer the question, "Who are we?" He sought to address the identity problems that had plagued the university since the 1980s merger era.

By the turn of the new millennium, CCU surged with optimism and promise—all this on the horizon: a new campus, growing programs with master's degrees, top-notch technology, and a community of students who were innovative outreach entrepreneurs before and after graduation.

1. Ron Schmidt, chapel address, January 7, 1997.

2. Jim McCormick, interview with the author, November 20, 2013.

3. The continuing education program took on various names, starting with Continuing Education for Teacher Certification and including the School of Professional Education ('90–'91), School of Innovative Studies

and School of Professional Studies ('91–'93), and Professional and Innovative Studies ('95–'96). Catalog changes occurred almost annually.

4. Larry Donnithorne, interview with Ken Gire, February 2, 2008. By the date of the Self-Study Report to the Higher Learning Commission, CCU claimed it owned 270 acres in Morrison.

CHAPTER 11

Strategies for a
New Millennium
2000–2014

The surge of energy and optimism for CCU at the beginning of the new millennium exhibited itself in growth and change. Residence hall space, which had been stretched to its limit, expanded when CCU broke ground for new apartments in early 2000. By August 11, just in time for the fall 2000 semester, CCU celebrated a ribbon cutting and welcomed the community into completed student housing. Eight months later, another residence hall was underway.

North Central Association approved CCU for a ten-year term of reaccreditation beginning in 2001, the longest accreditation term possible. Then, the university experienced a series of refocusing events. President Donnithorne initiated a series of administrative reorganizations in 2001, 2002, and 2003, which resulted in layoffs, combined or restructured services, and curricular reductions. At the same time, the post- 9/11 financial

President Larry Donnithorne. *From Graduation Foto.*

crisis caused strained purse strings and lower-than-expected enrollment growth.

One surprising administrative decision was the sale of KWBI and its daughter stations to K-LOVE, a nationwide Christian broadcasting network. KWBI, KJOL FM, and an FM translator co-owned with the KDRH network had a solid presence on the airwaves of Colorado, with familiar radio personalities. The transition took place at lightning speed, with a complete program shift from KWBI to K-LOVE on October 5, 2000.[1]

Public response was mixed, with many listener voices vehemently opposing the sale

KJOL.

alongside supporters who valued the youth-oriented outreach of K-LOVE. Final closing documents on the sale of the radio stations were signed in April of 2001 for

Students on Best of Colorado trip with Jim McCormick in 2001.

$16 million, and license agreements were sold in 2003 for an additional $2.5 million.

In 2001, the adult programs, formerly called the School of Professional Studies, underwent a radical restructuring. All staff members were laid off and asked to reapply for new positions in the new school. With a new name, the School of Adult and Graduate Studies began pulling together adult undergraduate programs, taught mostly in evening and weekend time slots, and graduate programs taught in-seat in various locations as well as online.

In the traditional undergraduate program, the layoffs deeply affected seven majors, eliminating two music majors, art, and physics, among others. The School of Music, Theater, and Arts and the School of Education were combined into the School of Education and Music from 2003 to 2006.

Long delays in the zoning hearings and frustrations about the Morrison property began to dampen the spirits of those seeking a new campus. In 2001, Dr. Donnithorne began exploring the Lockheed Martin facility near Deer Creek as a possible campus site. After rezoning applications were turn down or in the process of denial, the administration continued seeking other sites for a new campus.

As a Division II school in the Rocky Mountain Athletic Conference (RMAC), CCU offered students opportunities to compete at high levels. On April 15, 2002, the RMAC Council of Presidents voted thirteen to one to require two additional sports if a school did not offer football. This decision would challenge CCU, as the $1.4 million in athletics funding for programming and athletic scholarships already strained the budget.[2] In a grueling session with the board a year later, Donnithorne recommended CCU withdraw from RMAC and create a "robust intermural program." Instead, the CCU board stripped athletics to the bare minimum, offering less than one-third of the scholarship funding athletics previously had available and reducing many staff positions to part time.

Snowboarding Ministry.

Fatboys Homeless Ministry (now called Sojourners).

Women's soccer team in Costa Rica for a mission.

CCU Gains Decision in Equal Opportunity for State Aid

On November 5, 2004, CCU initiated a lawsuit against the State of Colorado to contest the constitutionality of a state agency's decision to exclude CCU students from state financial assistance. The Colorado Commission on Higher Education had rejected CCU's application to participate in state aid for needy students because it claimed CCU was "pervasively sectarian." CCU asked the Colorado legislature to "eliminate religious discrimination in the statutes governing the aid program," and CCU was denied its request.

CCU pursued a civil lawsuit that challenged the definition of the term "pervasively sectarian." The Alliance Defense Fund and the Christian Legal Society filed the lawsuit against the Colorado Commission on Higher Education on behalf of CCU.[3]

The case was resolved in 2009, when the Tenth U.S. Circuit Court of Appeals reversed a district court's ruling in favor of CCU.

One way the athletic program was able to survive and grow was through a dedication to mentor student-athletes spiritually. CCU athletes began their 2003 academic year by attending a retreat together, a first for CCU. Secondly, the inaugural Hall of Fame Banquet was held in October 2003, in which student-athletes served a fundraising dinner and honored CCU's athletic stars. By mid-decade, CCU developed men's baseball and women's golf, which drew more student-athletes to the university. In 2012, women's softball was added.

Information meetings, Town Hall meetings, and Christ-like dialogue assignments consumed some of the faculty and staff's energy from 2002 to 2005. Operating deficits resulting in layoffs and restructuring had posed part of the problem, but the administration also sought to address what it called the "noise" surrounding CCU's theological position. Some alumni and constituents charged CCU's theological position with "drifting" from an evangelical core, but others affirmed it as a "centering." "Lower the noise" meetings in 2004 and working groups in 2005 sought to dispel some of this discontent. These groups clarified that most of the discontent was the result of financial insecurity, programs vying

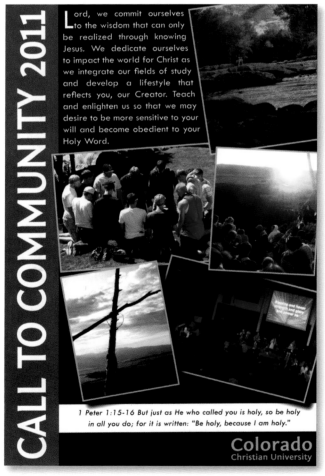

CALL TO COMMUNITY 2011

Lord, we commit ourselves to the wisdom that can only be realized through knowing Jesus. We dedicate ourselves to impact the world for Christ as we integrate our fields of study and develop a lifestyle that reflects you, our Creator. Teach and enlighten us so that we may desire to be more sensitive to your will and become obedient to your Holy Word.

1 Peter 1:15-16 But just as He who called you is holy, so be holy in all you do; for it is written: "Be holy, because I am holy."

Colorado Christian University

Call to Community is a tradition for new students and families during the Weekend of Welcome.

Student snowboarders, 2004.

for scarce resources, and unclear power structures.

Some programs marked solid success during this era—the master of business administration program graduated its first cohort in 2004. The master of counseling program re-opened its doors to a new class in 2003 after several years' hiatus. And

teacher education and music education programs were granted accreditation by the Association of Christian Schools in 2004.

Through many generous gifts, the Lost Boys of Sudan, so named because they were orphaned by the Second Sudanese Civil War, began attending CCU in 2004. Nine graduated, beginning in 2008.

The fiscal year ending July 2005 reported an operating surplus, and CCU's College of Undergraduate Studies reported a 10 percent increase in enrollment the fall of 2005, which brought great relief and some returning optimism.

With some of the discontent dispelled, President Donnithorne

Sons of Sudan.

Strategic Objectives

Colorado Christian University shall:

Honor Christ and share the love of Christ on campus and around the world;

Teach students to trust the Bible, live holy lives and be evangelists;

Be a magnet for outstanding students and prepare them for positions of significant leadership the church, business, government and professions by offering an excellent education in strategic disciplines;

Teach students how to learn;

Teach students how to think for themselves;

Teach students how to speak and write clearly and effectively;

Give students significant opportunities to serve our Lord while they are at CCU and to help them develop a lifetime habit of such service;

Impact our culture in support of traditional family values, right-to-life, biblical view of human nature, limited government, personal freedom, free markets, natural law, original intent of the Constitution, Western civilization;

Be seekers of truth;

Debunk "spent ideas" and those who traffic in them;

Ask God to multiply our time and ability to the glory of His great name;

Be a servant of the Church;

Become a great university.

President Bill Armstrong.

resigned in the spring of 2006. CCU's board lost no time in seeking a new presidential candidate and landed on Bill Armstrong who had retired from the U.S. Senate in 1991.

When CCU Board Chairman Bill White met with Armstrong to invite him to consider becoming a candidate for the position, Armstrong says he immediately thought, "What an honor. Do not do this thing!" Then as he met with key leaders seeking advice and direction, the strategic objectives of "a university that really honors Christ" emerged. He took these objectives to each of the board members individually to explain his understanding of them and to warn them that this countercultural stance would cause problems. Undeterred, the board elected Armstrong to begin his tenure in August of 2006.[4]

With a background in media, business, and finance, President Armstrong brings a high level of energy and business acumen to CCU. More importantly, he has an active personal ministry of evangelism and loves Jesus. He seeks to raise the profile of CCU in the Denver region and nationally by restoring the institution to its conservative Christian roots. President Armstrong envisions CCU becoming a great university, one that challenges spent ideas and promotes an education that calls Christians to action. He provided strategic objectives through which

A Magnet for Special Speakers

University-wide symposiums engage students in cross-discipline challenges, such as evangelism in 2010 and compassion for the poor in 2011. The Values Aligned Leadership Summit (VALS) draws business leaders to its annual spring gathering.

The Centennial Institute offers internships and programs, and the School of Music and the Department of Athletics draw artists and athletes for performances and fundraising events. The School of Theology offers debates and an Inklings Symposium celebrates C. S. Lewis's legacy. Chapel speakers often include nationally known Christian teachers and artists.

Among many others, CCU has hosted Congresswoman Michele Bachmann, Ambassador John Bolton, presidential candidate Herman Cain, Christian artist Michael Card, Senator Tom Coburn, Nixon presidential aide Chuck Colson, Senator Ted Cruz, Focus on the Family founder Dr. James Dobson, president and CEO of Samaritan's Purse Franklin Graham, former Governor Mike Huckabee, radio host Hugh Hewitt, author Jerry Jenkins, former Governor Dick Lamm, jazz artist Don Lanphere, composer Morten Lauridsen, poet Marilyn Chandler McEntyre, former Governor Sarah Palin, guitarist Christopher Parkening, Governor Rick Perry, radio talk show host Dennis Prager, former Governor Bill Ritter, Senator Rick Santorum, investigative reporter John Stossel, author and pastor Lee Strobel, Congressman Colonel Allen West, and bass trombonist Doug Yeo.

Symposium.

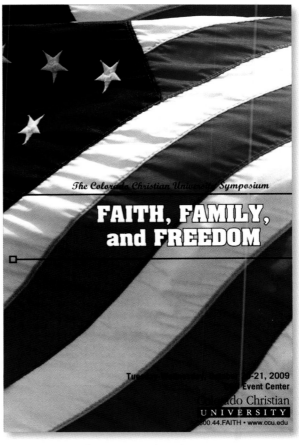

Symposium brochure.

CCU's mission could be accomplished (see sidebar). Themed programs such as the "Year of the Bible" and the "Year of Evangelism," along with symposiums, partnerships with local non-profits, and challenging special speakers open opportunities for students and friends of the university to learn the whys and hows of Christian commitment.

Dr. Beckman.

Armstrong took a fresh look at the Morrison property. A rezoning application already underway when Armstrong joined CCU, the November 2006 attempt would have pushed the campus northeast on the Morrison property and would have added residential platting in the western valley. For various reasons—the distance from jobs and transportation for students among them— Armstrong believed the Morrison property was not the right setting for the university. Armstrong engaged Shea Properties to assist CCU in applying for rezoning the property for high-quality housing, making the decision that the Morrison property would be used as an asset, not for campus development.

The resulting plans removed development of a campus from the rezoning application and divided the land into areas that included 280 cluster lots that preserved views, the wildlife corridor, and geological features of what would be called the Lyon's Ridge development. This third rezoning submittal in August 2007 raised community concerns that the plan did not meet South Jefferson County Community Plan guidelines. Finally, with the aid of

Shea Properties, CCU submitted a plan in January 2008 that required no Urban Growth Boundary amendments. The final platting would include 230 residential lots with open space. Jefferson County Commissioners J. Kevin McCasky, chair, and Jim Congrove courageously risked political fallout to vote in favor of CCU's rezoning. President Armstrong declared June 11, 2008, a day of praise and thanksgiving after the Jefferson County Board of Commissioners approved CCU's rezoning request.

CCU's heritage schools had been strongly involved with adult education from 1914 onwards through evening diploma programs offered by DBI and WBI. Colorado Baptist Junior College designed programs specifically for adult education from a Christian worldview, and Rockmont's programs in continuing education reached across Colorado, engaging adult learners.

About 2005, under the new name College of Adult and Graduate Studies (CAGS), administrators began to notice a transition in the target audience for adult

Above: VALS Panel.

Right: Students interact at VALS.

Above: Business students dress professionally on Thursdays.

Left: Students outside the Clifton Fowler Library.

CCU Commencement, 2013.

education. Until then, students sought to be "credentialed" for their life and work experiences and complete degrees that would help them advance professionally. After 2005, the target audience of students changed. They were younger and less experienced; they didn't want a degree completion program as much as a full, non-traditional university experience. They sought professional degrees, such as accounting, nursing, and business administration.

Online education significantly changed the face of CAGS as well, with 80 percent of the student population taking some classes online. Some students experience education purely online, while others choose among online, hybrid, and in-seat course offerings. CCU graduation has included soldiers graduating by simulcast from a deployment with a commanding officer shaking hands while the CCU community watches the big screen.

CCU has been at the forefront of adult education, and the visionary leadership of school founders and leaders prepared the way for the transformation that CAGS can make in individual student lives. They had the foresight to recognize that adults in the midst of busy lives need alternative educational models. CAGS operates at seven locations, plus Global Online, and offers four graduate programs, sixteen bachelor degrees, and seven associate degrees. With encouragement of CCU leadership, CAGS continues to be flexible and innovative, with a student success team that follows student engagement and persistence, advising students in career development. Committed to growing

CAGS opens new locations.

CAGS Services in Colorado Springs.

CAGS Building in Colorado Springs.

adult students into world changers, CAGS sponsors learning and service trips around the world, including a nursing program trip to Costa Rica Dr. Barbara White and her husband sponsored in 2012.

Demolition makes way for new campus development.

Campus Re-Development

After securing the rezoning of the Morrison property, which was platted and ready for sale, CCU's administration again faced the problem of how to increase facilities to allow for growth. Much consideration was given to regional properties, but none met CCU's vision. In 2011, President Armstrong and the board of trustees agreed the Lakewood campus should be redeveloped.

President Armstrong and his consultants held meetings with City of Lakewood officials, neighborhood groups, staff and faculty, and student groups. The new campus design is projected to cost more than $120 million, with $55 million expected from charitable gifts, and will be conducted in phases as funds are available.[5]

Phase One is underway in the 2013–2014 academic year, including an academic building which will house state-of-the-art classrooms, a multi-purpose hall, faculty offices, a student lounge, and a study hall for CCU's next generation of World Changers.

New academic building, 2014.

Artist rendering of campus development.
From the 2012–2013 CCU Annual Report.

Campus site plan.

Junkyard Stairwell.

The College of Undergraduate Studies (CUS) offers two semesters of courses in seventy-five-minute blocks, Monday to Thursday. Students attend chapel twice each week. Yetter, Harwood, and Waite Halls house freshman stairwells, but because of growth, some freshmen also live in the residence halls called the Peaks. Following the traditions of the early heritage schools, students volunteer in the community a total of 180 hours over four years.

In a report to the Colorado Commission on Higher Education dated January 12, 2005, President Donnithorne had numbered CCU students at 2,962.[6] With the additions of CAGS students numbering in the thousands and growth of CUS in the hundreds, the fall of 2013 reports a student body of 5,307—4,197 in CAGS and 1,110 in CUS.

Beginning in 2009, administrators, faculty, and staff began a process of self-

Centennial Institute

CCU President Bill Armstrong founded the Centennial Institute and named former Colorado Senate President John Andrews as director. Centennial Institute is funded from private contributions, and it sponsors research, publications, and events. It exists as a non-partisan "think tank to enhance public understanding of issues relating to 'faith, family, and freedom' and to renew the spirit of 1776."[7] At the time of the institute's founding, Andrews also hosted *Backbone Radio* and contributed to the *Denver Post* and television programs. Additionally, he served as a state senator from 1998 to 2005. He had founded the Independence Institute, one of the first state-based, free market think tanks, and was its president from 1985 to 1993.

The Centennial Institute publishes a series of policy briefs for legislators and *Centennial Review*, a digest of speeches from CCU events. It hosts Issue Monday (a monthly forum) and the Western Conservative Summit. One of the institute's core activities includes mentoring the 1776 scholars, a group of twelve to twenty students, during their four-year academic life. Student learning experiences include introducing speakers, hosting VIP dinners, and conducting research. Mentoring students deeply connects the institute to CCU while it advances public debate and discussion of the great issues of the day in Colorado and the nation.

study to prepare the school for a 2011 reaccreditation visit. What was the result? The North Central Association awarded CCU another ten-year reaccreditation.

CCU is committed to spiritual transformation, and classes in CUG and CAGS

John Andrews, Centennial Institute.

Alyssa Silkwood with Colonel Allen West at the Western Conservative Summit in 2013.

incorporate biblical aspects of a discipline and examine how to learn a subject with a foundation of faith. Learning means doing, and each year student leadership opportunities abound. Student-led CCU2theWorld trips take

the gospel across several continents. Over the past twelve years, students have led more than two hundred teams to fifty countries and twelve states. CAGS teams have traveled to China and South Africa.

CCU2theWorld in Jamaica.

CAGS students travel to South Africa.

1. In "Vantage Point," his letter to alumni and friends, President Donnithorne explained the abrupt change was necessary because KWBI's Sharathon fundraiser was imminent and it would be disingenuous to proceed with the fundraiser when the radio station was under negotiated sale. *Vantage* 2.2 (Winter 2000), 3.

2. Eric Palmer, "Donnithorne Announces Athletics Plans," *Cougar Trax*, 11.5 (October 29, 2002), 1.

3. Amber Stroud, *Cougar Trax* (October 3, 2006), 3, 6; Charity Joy Gustafson, *Cougar Trax* (February 22, 2009), 2–3.

4. Bill Armstrong, interview with the author and Cherri Parks, November 26, 2013.

5. Vanessa Jackson, "On the Horizon: Campus Changes for CCU," *Veritas* IV, no.4 (December 8, 2011), 1.

6. Larry Donnithorne, Colorado Commission on Higher Education, Report of Private Colleges and Universities Operating in Colorado under the Degree Authorization Act, January 12, 2005.

7. Haley Littleton, "Think Tank at CCU: Centennial Institute," *Veritas* IV, no. 2 (October 5, 2010), 1.

CHAPTER 12
World Changers

Harold Ogilvie '18 DBI

Harold Ogilvie was among the first graduates of DBI. Viola, his wife, was also a DBI student. Ogilvie had been the director of the DBI program "Hope of Israel Mission" in Denver, an outreach to Jewish immigrants. DBI students assisted Ogilvie in conducting Sunday School, gospel services, and industrial classes for children. Ogilvie was the first of many foreign missionaries to go through DBI's program, serving in 1921 in Nigeria under Sudan Interior Mission.

By 1935, Ogilvie had translated two-thirds of the New Testament into Irigwe and was revising the Hausa Bible. Ogilvie trained new missionaries at a SIM language school at Jos, teaching Hausa.[1] When on furlough, the Ogilvies served churches, such as the First Baptist Church of Longmont, Colorado, and they helped Carl C. Harwood and Clarence Harwood with ministries to servicemen in Denver during World War II. After he retired, Ogilvie continued preaching and was involved in planting new churches, including the Grace Baptist Church near Daytona Beach, Florida, in 1966.

The Ogilvies, 1923. *Courtesy of H. A. and Christine Wilson and now part of the CCU archive.*

Clarence Harwood '28 DBI

Clarence Harwood excelled in business, and his ministry heart was always for the Jewish people, trying to show them who the true Messiah was in their lives. Harwood recruited his brother Carl to be a student at DBI, and he was just as fun to be around. He and Carl founded a ministry to servicemen in Denver during World War II, and they founded the Spurgeon Foundation to support evangelism. After Clarence and his son Stan sold Purity Creamery, Clarence sold investments. His commitment to Bible training resulted in his family's donation of land to WBI in 1959, and he recruited his children and grandchildren in the enterprise. Several granddaughters even worked on drywall to get the new campus ready for students. One granddaughter and her husband attended WBI, another worked in the library, his grandson did engineering for the radio station, and Clarence's daughter-in-law Betty Harwood worked for KWBI.[2]

Clarence Harwood. *Courtesy of Rodene Harwood.*

Ernest E. Lott '33 DBI and Annie (Martin) Lott '34 DBI

When he first graduated from DBI, Ernest Lott dove headfirst into DBI's ministries. By 1934, he served as the director of evangelism, arranging for students to conduct street evangelism and run programs in the Denver area; taught Modern Religions; travelled with the Faculty Men's Quartet; contributed articles and columns to *Grace and Truth*; and managed the Book Nook. Toward the end of his tenure at DBI, he served as editor of *Grace and Truth* and was secretary of the DBI Board. Annie Lott was writing columns for *Grace and Truth*.

Ernest Lott.

Putting others before himself, Lott was a steady worker who relieved others from tedious duties. For instance, he took over Clifton Fowler's expositions on the International Sunday School Lesson, writing this curriculum aid for years. In the difficult years when Fowler's divorce discredited DBI's education among conservatives, Lott persevered and filled in where needed:

teaching, music leadership, administration, printing, conference and camp ministry, class sponsorship, and broadcasting.

Lott left DBI in 1943 after more than ten years of ministry to join Back to the Bible in Lincoln, Nebraska. There, he worked in publishing and broadcasting for founder Theodore Epp, reaching an even wider national audience. He also served on the boards of Maranatha Bible Camp (Nebraska), Kings Engineering Fellowship (Iowa), Berean Mission Society (Missouri), and his home church in Lincoln, Nebraska.

Ivan Olsen '36 DBI

When Michigan native Ivan Olsen sought Bible training, he wrote to Rueben Lindquist at DBI. He saved that letter, noting all expenses to the penny and exposing the basic supplies he was not able to afford when he arrived. Olsen was

president of DBI's Student Organization and student pastor of five rural churches in Colorado.[3] When he graduated in 1936, Fowler recommended Olsen to a new church in North Platte, Nebraska, and they elected him pastor, sight unseen.[4] He led Bible studies in surrounding towns, and as these groups started their own churches, he coordinated a fellowship of churches in 1947. He is known as the founder of the Berean Fellowship of Churches.

In 1938, Olsen began Maranatha Bible Camp in Maxwell, Nebraska, and served as director for more than fifty years. He drew deeply from his relationships with DBI students and faculty to maintain this ministry.

William R. Read '49 Rockmont and Lenore (Smith) Read '45 DBI, '46 DBC

A member of returning World War II veterans, Bill Read met Lenore at what was to become Rockmont College. He and others like him had their eyes opened to a world of opportunities while at war, and these

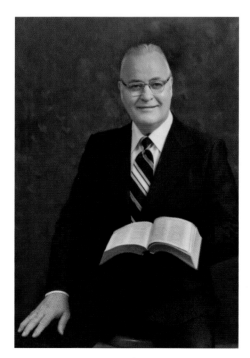

Ivan Olsen.

Rockmont students conduct street evangelism in the 1940s.

young students were innovative evangelists before they ever graduated. In the early days, DBI students had a place outside a laundry for street preaching. By the 1940s, these returning servicemen, whose hearts were full of enthusiasm for evangelism, worked the streets of Denver until late in the evening. Lenore tells the story of one student, Bob Lahr, who was expelled when he stayed out after curfew too many times. Bill and his friends were part of the Gospel Bombardiers, who rolled gospel tracks in cellophane and dropped them from the airspace over Denver.

Bill and Lenore served for seventeen years as missionaries in Brazil, then in pastorates in Denver and Arizona. He became the home mission director for the Presbyterian Church in America and the home and foreign mission director for the Evangelical Presbyterian Church.

Tom Graham '50 Rockmont and Eleanor (Hayes) Graham '50 Rockmont

Tom met Eleanor at Rockmont, as he says, "by divine providence and the alphabetical seating chart." In January of their senior year, they married. While attending various graduate schools and settling into careers, they raised three children, Nathan, Daniel, and Joy. Eleanor put her Bible training to good use by serving children in many church positions and leading Good News clubs. Professionally, she worked for twenty-two years as a teacher aide with special education junior high students. For thirty-four years, Tom served in various positions at California State University in Los Angeles: professor, department chair, dean,

Tom and Eleanor Graham. *Courtesy of Tom Graham.*

and international director for the UK study abroad program.

Early in his career, Tom and others developed an assessment model for the United States Peace Corps at a time when tens of thousands of applicants were vying for positions. When their son Daniel was seriously injured in a motorcycle accident in 1982, Tom temporarily took an early retirement from the university to care for him. At the same time, Tom founded the Center for Organizational and Ministry Development in 1983, which assists organizations with leadership and growth in ways similar to his Peace Corps work. His organization has assisted with thousands of ministry domestic and international placements over the years.

William P. "Billy" Renstrom '51 WBI

Serving in General Patton's Third Army in France during World War II, Billy Renstrom was sent out in charge of thirteen men to clear up a German mine field. In one brief, tragic incident, Renstrom accidentally snagged a mine he was dragging to safety when he was only about twenty feet away. When he came to, he could not see.

Billy Renstrom. *Courtesy of Ruby Renstrom.*

Renstrom enrolled in DBC and then transferred to WBI soon after it was founded. He was among the first graduates of WBI in 1951. Ruby Harwood, President Harwood's daughter, was his reader, and although she didn't graduate from WBI, she received a full education. They married, and he worked at WBI for several years.

In addition to his WBI duties, Renstrom pastored a church in Boone, Colorado, for two years. He then worked as associate pastor of Central Bible Church in Denver before joining the ministry of Bill Rice, a nationally known evangelist and the founder of a large camp for the deaf in Murfreesboro, Tennessee.

By 1975, new procedures had developed for Renstrom's blindness, and he underwent surgery, waking up to partially restored vision. Phoning his wife from his hospital room, Renstrom relayed the good news ironically by complaining of the garish colors of the pajamas that his wife had selected. For the first time, he was able to see the faces of his children.

In 1980, Renstrom and his wife formed their own evangelistic team, and he later served as associate pastor of a Baptist church in Florida. Blindness once again overtook him as he struggled with illnesses toward the end of his life. Renstrom died in 2012 after sixty-four years of ministry.

Daniel Ee '64 WBI

Danny Ee attended a Youth for Christ (YFC) camp in his native Singapore where

Danny Ee. *Courtesy of Elsie Fick and now part of the CCU archive.*

a missionary from Denver, Don Whipple '55 Rockmont, challenged him to prepare for ministry at WBI. Whipple contacted WBI president Carl Harwood Jr. who helped arrange a generous scholarship for Danny.

After graduation in 1964, Ee returned to Singapore to work with YFC, serving for fifteen years. He directed the Singapore YFC and founded the Hong Kong YFC. Later, he was director of Asian affairs and was evangelist at large for YFC International. His heart was in evangelism. In the spring and early summer of 1978, Ee led international YFC rallies accompanied by a musical group of thirty-four young musicians whom he trained to be counselors. He travelled with the team to Australia and Hong Kong, where despite a typhoon, they held rallies and presented programs in prisons. In six weeks alone, Ee preached to 36,000 people and his team counseled 568 young people, many of whom made first-time decisions to follow Christ. He also set up follow-up programs with local churches.[5]

In 1981, Ee returned to WBC to serve in admissions and evangelism, and he fulfilled his dream of presenting WBC to "pastors, youth pastors, servicemen, and especially high school graduates and those who are wanting to prepare themselves for the ministry."[6] Then he rejoined YFC and founded work in Honolulu, Hawaii.

Arturo Kinch '79 Rockmont

From a large mission family in Costa Rica, Arturo Kinch participated in basketball, soccer, and downhill skiing at Rockmont. He graduated with degrees in biblical studies and camping and

Arturo Kinch.

recreation. Arturo did not aim at being a top skier at Rockmont but was merely using the sport to keep in shape for soccer. But he was a natural, and he was the ski team's top point scorer for several seasons. In order to compete internationally, Kinch learned he must be a member of his national ski association, so he founded the Costa Rica Ski Association and became the first Olympic athlete from Costa Rica in the sport. From his first Olympics—Lake Placid in 1980—to Salt Lake in 2002, Kinch competed in alpine skiing for a country that had no snow. In 1984 (Sarajevo), Kinch also competed in cross-country skiing and continued in that sport at age forty-nine at the 2006 Olympics in Torino. In 2004, Kinch was inducted into CCU's Hall of Fame.

John and Jenny Haines.

John Haines '83 Rockmont

John Haines and Jenny (Warfield) Haines '83 married during their senior year of college. Haines attributes his Rockmont-style of education—personal attention and a high level of semi-professional experience—to his gaining a place at the prestigious Eastman School of Music, University of Rochester. Currently, he is director of worship at the 2,000-member Christ Covenant Church in Charlotte, North Carolina, where he oversees several choirs and an orchestra and is in charge of the liturgy. He is also the director of the Institute for Sacred Music, a graduate training program in partnership with Reformed Theological Seminary and St. Andrews Theological College and Seminary.

Haines has been a guest speaker and conducted master classes at the Hajibeyov Baku Academy of Music in Azerbaijan, and he wrote a symphonic suite for the birthday anniversary of composer Uzeyir Hajibeyov. John and Jenny raised four children while gaining academic credentials:

John a doctorate in theology and Jenny a PhD in marriage and family therapy. Jenny is an assistant professor and director of the Pfeiffer Institute for Marriage and Family Therapy at Pfeiffer University in Charlotte, North Carolina.

Greg Stier '88 CCC

Founder and president of Dare 2 Share, a ministry to teens, Greg Stier calls himself a "twitchy revolutionary." After watching his tough, urban family transformed as they came to Christ, Stier knew he was going to be a preacher by the time he was about eleven years old. Stier has filled amphitheaters and talked with more than one million teens over his twenty-plus years of ministry. He motivates young people to form relationships with others to reach out to them with the transforming gospel. Stier equips teens to act on their

Greg Stier.

faith. In addition, he has authored fifteen books, appeared on national television, and partnered with international ministries. He writes, "Our world today is filled with many good and worthy causes, but the cause that consumed Jesus is the ultimate cause! His cause is THE Cause...to make disciples who make disciples."[7]

Scott Miller.

Scott Miller '91 CCU

Starting at Interstate Batteries at age fourteen, Scott Miller began by sweeping the floors and now is CEO and president of the company. He bills Interstate as a Christian company that values the Golden Rule and biblical values, to which he ascribes Interstate's success. He carries on the legacy of his father, Norm Miller, who had been president and chairman of the board. Interstate is the number one replacement brand battery in North America and is a more than $1 billion, privately held company. It recycles more lead than any other single entity in the

United States. Innovative marketing techniques marked its rise to being a household name, such as sponsoring for thirteen years a vintage car rally through Italy, radio advertising on Paul Harvey, and sponsoring championship fishermen and NASCAR.

Interstate's corporate culture is equally innovative. Interstate declares its "unabashed mission to conduct business in a way that honors God" and offers a corporate chaplain and staff and opportunities for employees to study the Bible, pray, and participate in Christian missions. Miller said when he attended CCU, his eyes were opened to the ways other businesses operated, and he realized what he experienced at Interstate was a better way to run a business.[8]

G. Michael Byrd '93 CCU

A retired veteran of the U.S. Air Force, Mike Byrd owns Allegiance Consulting Inc., a staffing company for IT and project managers and fills many government contracts. Before founding this business, he worked as a director of global training for

Mike Byrd.

Amy Beth (Larson) Barlow.

Compassion International, which operates in twenty-seven countries. From 1994 to 2000, he was center director of the CCU Colorado Springs campus and continues to teach CCU graduate and undergraduate classes in leadership, management, and communications, now mostly online. He was a training facilitator for NORAD and the United States Northern Command/ Homeland Defense. He has previously served as an education and training manager for the U.S. Air Force at Schriever Air Force Base, Colorado.

Mike also has been instrumental in local church administration. He served on staff at Woodmen Valley Chapel (Colorado Springs) and he and his wife Donna attend Harvest Bible Chapel (Denver). He has also taught leadership development at Harvest Bible Chapel's School of Ministry

in Chicago, Illinois, to pastors who are planting new churches at thirty-seven different locations.

Amy Beth (Larson) Barlow '95 CCU

Through charity work, West Side Ministries began as a student-run CCU outreach and became official in 1993 with CCU students committing to work in several Denver west-side neighborhoods. It facilitates Bible clubs, tutoring, mentoring, music camp, and summer clubs for at-risk kids. In 2002, it added EDGG (Everything Done to the Glory of God) for junior and senior high school students involving discipleship, mentoring, and service.[9] The Third Story is an outgrowth of West Side Ministries, and it functions as a non-profit with a press and the Sound Lot, a storytelling and music ministry "to educate listeners about the realities and needs in our inner city neighborhoods and share the stories that are born there."[10] This small

ministry has a leader with a big heart, and she has inspired urban children and CCU student volunteers to follow Jesus.

1. Jim Mason, *Literature Outreach in Nigeria: A History of SIM Literature Work 1901- 1980* (Scarborough, Ontario: SIM Canada, 2009), 160.

2. Rodene "Dee" Harwood, phone conversation with author, November 27, 2013.

3. Elmer Seger, "In the Harvest Field," *G&T* (October 1935), 285.

4. Ivan E. Olsen, "The History of the Berean Fundamental Church Council, Inc., The Berean Fellowship," (September 10, 1979), http://www.colbyberean.com/HistoryBereanFellowship.pdf, accessed November 8, 2013.

5. "Alumni News," *Western Witness* (August 1978), 4.

6. "New Faces in the 'Family: Danny Ee Returns to Alma Mater as Admissions Director," *Western Witness* (Spring 1981), 3, 8.

7. "Founder," dare2share.org, "My Story," gregstier.org, and "The Cause," gregStier.org, accessed November 28, 2013.

8. Nicholas Sakelaris, "Scott Miller Carries Interstate Batteries' Family Legacy," *Dallas Business Journal* (March 15, 2013); "Interstate History and Milestones," and "Corporate Chaplain," corporate.interstatebatteries.com, accessed November 29 2013; Steven R. Thompson, "Scott Miller Climbed the Ladder at Interstate Batteries Independent from His Chairman Father," *The Business Journals* (February 24, 2012).

9. Amy Beth Larson, "West Side Ministries Gets EDGGy," *Cougar Trax* 11.1 (August 22, 2002), 5.

10. "Third Story Sound Lot," thethirdstory.org, accessed November 29, 2013.

EPILOGUE

The Next 100 Years
by William Armstrong, President of CCU

President Armstrong.

In many ways, Colorado Christian University is like other colleges and universities. CCU has long been nationally accredited. The university offers both graduate and undergraduate degrees. We have traditional, adult, and graduate students; classrooms; syllabi; faculty; fundraising; sports teams; a tree-lined campus, student residences, etc.

But our heart is very different from most institutions of higher education. We champion a conservative point of view in theology, lifestyle, economics, culture, and patriotism. Our faculty, staff, and most students hold a traditional understanding of human nature, right versus wrong, and the authority of the Bible.

We are deeply concerned about recent national trends including the breakup of families, sexual permissiveness, drug abuse, the stifling effects of big government, high taxes and regulation, abuse of power by the judiciary, disrespect of traditional values, and ignorance of Western Civilization.

Our ideals are in stark contrast with the liberal dogma of schools where Jesus is denigrated, the Bible is treated as irrelevant, sexual promiscuity is tolerated or encouraged, and drunkenness, recreational drug use, and bad manners are prevalent. At such "politically correct" schools, students are fed a diet of left-wing notions about life, culture, economics, and politics.

By standing up to be counted for Jesus, the Bible, traditional values, sanctity of life, free markets, natural law, original intent of the Constitution (and much more), CCU upholds the opinions of tens of millions of Americans for whom faith, family, and freedom are bedrock values. By doing so, CCU affords students a rare opportunity for high-quality education, exploration of the depth and breadth of crucial ideas, and great academic traditions, all steeped in the love of Christ.

CCU Debate Team, 2013.

CCU is different from other universities in another important respect—truth in packaging. Most schools fall somewhere on the spectrum from liberal to ultra-liberal, as documented by the American Council of Trustees and Alumni, the National Association of Scholars, and numerous surveys of faculty attitudes. Often, however, they conceal their culture and ingrained values and pretend to be something they are not.

CCU must never do this. More than ever before, as we begin our second century, we hear God calling Colorado Christian University to greatness, to be uncompromising in our testimony and teaching. Let us pray to be filled with the Holy Spirit and the power to answer His call in every day of the next one hundred years.

CCU students at Weekend of Welcome in 2012.

INDEX

ABOUT THE AUTHOR

Dr. Janet M. Black is an associate professor of English and chair of the Department of English at CCU. She lives in Lakewood, Colorado, with her family.